RE-CREATING THE *World*

THE POWER AND JOY OF COLLABORATIVE CREATIVITY

DR. LISA A. KRAMER

Re-Creating The World: The Power and Joy of Collaborative Creativity
Copyright © 2023 Lisa A. Kramer

Editing, design, and distribution by Bublish
Published by Spark Collaborative Media
ISBN: 979-8-988089-01-8 (eBook)
ISBN: 979-8-988089-00-1 (paperback)

Dedicated to all the dreamers, the seekers
the creators, and the doers
who strive together
for more creative ways to heal our world.

CONTENTS

PART 1
DISCOVERING CREATIVE SPARKS

CHAPTER 1

All it takes is a spark. Strike a match; a flame flashes. It can turn into a controlled fire in a fireplace, a dancing and sparkling bonfire, or a wildfire that consumes acres of trees. Fire contains everything: beauty, danger, purification, destruction, and the power of rebirth. When fire destroys, it makes room for something new to begin. Building something new on the foundation of something else is creativity.

Creativity starts with a spark, but not in the way many people think. Creative ideas do not always appear like lightning strikes in swift moments of inspiration. Sometimes it can happen like that, but that's actually pretty rare. If you wait for lightning to strike before you even begin, you may be waiting a long time.

A spark is tiny, but that's all that is necessary. The tiniest seed can grow into the tallest tree. Imagine that you happen to be listening to a lecture by a speaker who seems to drone on . . . and on . . . and on. You lose interest in what he is saying and doodle along the edges of your notebook, taking down words and phrases here and there. For some reason, he mentions the word *pirate*, so you jot that word in the margin, which leads you to writing down phrases in pirate talk.

"Arr, matey. What be this lubber dronin' on about?"

Suddenly, you find your mind wandering into a memory of a dream you once had—one in which you were the pirate captain of a ship on the open sea, bravely leading your crew on adventures of all kinds. You find yourself doodling images of that dream in the margins, no longer even attempting to take notes. Lines form stick figures, not very skilled but bringing your vision to life. Later that day, you can't get the sketch out of your mind. You start exploring the idea in different ways: drawing, painting, studying pirate phrases, researching the history of different pirates while listening to pirate songs.

This leads to you writing a blog post on the history of piracy, then a short story, and then turning it into a script, until the collaborative peak of producing a movie with other creative people. This movie then sparks new possibilities with the dreamers who sit in the audience, inspiring them to sail, to solve the problem of modern-day piracy, to build new types of boats, or even to clean the oceans. It all started with that small spark, that tiny word that joined with other ideas and people until you had an amazing collective flame that burned across the world.

A spark can appear at unexpected moments when you are interacting with other people. It can come from a subtle message, a conversation, a laugh, a shared idea, or a simple suggestion. Amazing things happen when we collectively strike matches and bring sparks to life *together*. Problems are solved, relationships are healed or built, collective challenges are overcome, and perceptions are changed. This collective power of creative energy brings warmth, light, or much-needed change to the world. This book is about the power of that collaborative creativity.

Pirate Spark by Danielle Williams

CHAPTER 2

Discovering the Need for Creative Collaboration

For much of my career, I have been an educator. Whether it was teaching English conversation in Japan, working with children in theater camps and leadership workshops, or teaching in college classrooms, I have always incorporated creative approaches with the interests and goals of the students in mind. I never really thought of myself as a teacher as much as a co-learner and mentor who helped bring diverse ideas and goals together.

In terms of subjects, I was teaching theater, theater history, acting, improvisation, writing, research, education, interdisciplinary studies, honors, and many other things. However, in terms of life skills, I've been teaching people:

- How to communicate across differences
- How to think beyond limitations in order to develop new ideas
- How to collaborate with others
- How to achieve goals in a timely manner

- How to adapt when the unexpected happens
- How to enjoy the process by tapping into their own creativity and ideas

In other words, my teaching and mentoring have always been less about the topics of the classes and more about what it means to be human in a complex, challenging, and ever-changing world. I was always seeking ways to make change by encouraging both individual and collaborative acts of creativity that bring people together across disciplines.

My process involves encouraging people to question things when they don't make sense and to strive to understand one another better. I incorporate ideas from different cultures and communities and works from outside a traditional Western canon. In liberal studies and interdisciplinary courses, I encouraged my more linear thinkers—like scientists and mathematicians—to understand and discover creative ways to communicate important information. I encouraged businesspeople to look beyond the numbers and recognize how creative work feeds an economy. I challenged people from criminal justice to see the world through the eyes of empathy and creativity so as to hopefully fight for more equitable and truly just systems. In every class, I asked people to work with those they thought they never had anything in common with, and they discovered what connects them with each other.

As chaos began to build around us during the COVID-19 lockdown, and people got angry in their silos of thought and politics, I realized one of the missing elements to finding solutions was the tool of working creatively across values and disciplines. We cannot find solutions for climate change unless we work at the intersections of science, sociology, economics, education, and public health (to name a few). We cannot fight poverty, racism, and inequality until we bring together people from opposing sides and perspectives, not to fight but to work with ideas in ways that build and grow rather than block and limit. I began to think about how I could help these collaborations happen.

CHAPTER 3

During the early days of the COVID-19 pandemic, everything changed for me, as it did for so many people. While my life was indeed touched by the sadness and loss, I found inspiration and new understanding about my own journey. As I faced the challenges of adapting, shifting, and discovering new approaches to work, play, and what it means to be a member of an interconnected world, I realized it was time for me to re-create my own path and help others do that as well.

At the time, I was teaching a class called Applied Theatre and Community Engagement at Worcester State University. I hold an MFA in theater directing and a PhD in theater for young audiences (with a focus on theater for social change), which took me on an eclectic career as either adjunct or visiting faculty in many different departments. Over the years, I discovered my passion lies in how theater, the arts in general, and creativity can be used as tools to promote social justice, inspire nontraditional thinking, challenge societal norms, and make real change. This course came about because of that passion.

It was intended to be a public-facing course, in which students learned techniques from improvisation and theater for social change, which they would apply to real-world situations.

Their final project was meant to be developing workshops, which they would lead for three groups from the larger community: two groups of young adults with severe learning and physical disabilities and a group of young adult new immigrants, some of whom did not speak much English and had left difficult situations behind. When everything shut down, the entire faculty had about one week to reconfigure our classes into something that could be done virtually, without losing any value.

My years of working, directing, and teaching in theater had taught me how to adapt when things don't go as expected. Since I always approached my classes as collaborations of sorts, where we cocreated what we would learn and achieve, my students and I found a way to create something wonderful, even in these extreme circumstances.

During that long semester and beyond, I found myself connecting with people from all around the world. I played games and laughed in virtual rooms. I witnessed a generous outpouring of creative work from artists of all types as they attempted to make the world feel more connected, even when we had to stay at least six feet apart. I heard songs sung across neighborhoods in Italy, intended to build a sense of community and togetherness where so many were confined alone.

This, I thought. *This is the power of collaborative creativity.*

And so . . . I began to write.

What you now hold in your hands is the product of that epiphany.

CHAPTER 4

How to Move through These Pages

Let's start with the premise that there are no rules to creativity, and nothing is perfect. In a world where people often judge their own creative ability by whether or not they are skilled at something, rules tend to be limiting in many ways. In the same way, perfectionism and the desire to do things "right" tend to limit the flow of creativity. While it often helps to understand rules before you break them, this is not a book about that. I'm not going to tell you how to structure your sentences. I won't teach you all the rules of specific art forms. Instead, in this book, I will explain different aspects of creativity, their importance, and how they can be applied in creative endeavors as well as beyond.

In each of these sections, I will also provide suggestions and offer prompts that can lead you in creative directions—directions that start with individual acts and grow into collaborative conversations. I won't tell you there is only one approach to collaborative creativity. Rather, through Inspired Actions, I offer you opportunities to play, explore, discover, and find answers to your own struggles and questions. I share my personal guidelines only so you can apply them *if they work for you*. You don't need my permission to create; all you need is your own. All you need is that spark. My hope is that you find it here.

Adopt a "Yes, And . . ." Philosophy

I use this one guiding philosophy whenever I lead workshops about creativity. One of the foundations of improvisation in theater is the concept of "Yes, And . . ." At its most basic level, in improv, this is the idea that you take whatever someone says or offers and build on it. In the hands of weak improvisers— those who care more about getting a cheap laugh than making their partners look good—the results are often less about collaboration and more about one-upmanship. But in the hands of strong improvisers—those who are most creative and care about making everyone involved feel good—the application of this philosophy leads to:

- Discovering new or interesting approaches
- Allowing space for all voices
- Expanding options in problem-solving that can lead to better solutions

When we adopt a Yes, And . . . philosophy, it allows us to accept possibilities and build on ideas without limiting ourselves or others. The true strength of this concept lies in accepting the gift of what is offered and helping that idea grow. It does not mean we have to agree with the gift but that we take it, accept it, and add to it or shift it in some way so the story continues. In terms of improvisation, hard noes or immediately killing someone off means a scene can't continue. Yet if we take an awkward offer and turn it into something positive, the scene moves forward, and we discover interesting solutions and relationships. For example, consider this possible beginning to an improvised scene:

Improvisor A: That's a cool old building. Let's go check it out.

Improvisor B: (*who happens to be in a wheelchair*) My wheelchair won't fit in the door, and I really don't want to be dragged up the steps.

Improvisor A: Oh yeah. I wonder if they have another entrance.

This scene could lead to an exploration of challenges that people with disabilities face or the creation of an easier way to give access.

The concept of Yes, And . . . moves beyond theater. What would happen if we embraced the concept in our lives, our businesses, and our relationships or as we try to come up with solutions to some of the bigger issues that plague us, like the environment, racism, and social justice? What would happen if the offer we received enabled us to find our own solutions to problems we didn't even realize existed? What would happen if you and your team said, "Yes, And . . ." to every idea in a brainstorming session? Imagine the possibilities.

Below are five reasons to adopt a Yes, And . . . philosophy:

- **Yes, And . . . expands your thinking beyond per-ceived limitations.** Whether you are brainstorm-ing an idea for your team or figuring out the next step of your own project, spending some time in the world of Yes, And . . . allows you to imagine all possibilities. Yes, sometimes things become impractical or unrealistic, and new ideas develop in that area where we ignore limitations and let our minds wander freely. For example, "These ideas are great, but we have a limited budget to help us launch our sustainable ideas podcast, and we have a large network of supporters on social media who could help spread the word."

- **Yes, And . . . gives you a new footing when things seem bad.** You lost your job, or your project was a failure, or a new law threatens to limit your freedoms. It's easy to fall into a slump and give up. However, if you change that negative into a new beginning—an offering you don't like but can build on—it may lead you in interesting directions. Yes, I lost my job, and now I have time to imagine myself in a new position. Yes, my project didn't work out the way I had hoped, and now I know how to do it better and be more successful. Yes, this law is horrible, and it will help us get more people to vote.

- **Yes, And . . . helps you connect with others.** Perhaps you are an introvert and don't like speaking in a room full of strangers but have to go to a social gathering. Or you are on a first date and trying to get through that getting-to-know-you stage. If you embrace the idea of Yes, And . . . it may help you find a way into connecting with others. Again, this does not mean you are agreeing with everything said. Rather, you are accepting statements as gifts and moving the conversation forward. For example, your date says, "I absolutely love seafood." That's the gift or the prompt. Your response could be something like "Interesting, for me it depends on how it's prepared. Have you ever tried sushi?" Note that you don't have to use the words *yes, and*, and you can use the word *no*; it's simply about receiving the idea and expanding on it.

- **Yes, And . . . encourages you to experience new things.** You are visiting a city you are unfamiliar with. You get lost on the way to the expensive and well-known restaurant your friend recommended. You wander around, stomach rumbling, unable to find anyone who can help you. Then you pass by a tiny hole-in-the-wall restaurant that seems to be filled with smiling, happy local people. The scents wafting out are intriguing. What do you do? Yes, And . . . would suggest that you take a chance on the local restaurant. You might discover something amazing. Allowing our feet to wander and our minds to discover something unexpected enables us to be open for the joys of travel and life, and thus more creativity.

- **Yes, And . . . always asks you to grow, learn, discover, change, and adapt when appropriate.** We all get set in our ways. Our way of thinking. Our way of doing things. By simply being open to receiving the gift of new perspectives and ideas, we, as individuals and collaborators, might just be able to find new solutions to the problems that challenge us today. All it takes is a willingness to try.

The one thing I ask of you, then, is that you Yes, And . . . your way through these pages. By doing so, you will unlock the full value of this book as well as your own potential.

Take Inspired Action

There is so much possibility when utilizing creativity in response to the world around us, as well as the circumstances and the people who inspire us. This is the ultimate power of a creative act—a call-and-response with the world. Throughout the book, I offer some Inspired Actions you can take. Do them as you wish. Discover your own approaches. Whenever possible, try to share the experience with other people because sharing with others is part of the power of collaborative creativity.

But Also, Procrastinate

I have one last, possibly radical, suggestion. Give yourself permission to procrastinate. Take time to move through this book and these exercises.

I know that goes against what everyone says about getting things done. For example, here's a quote from Anthony Iannarino, a coach who "helps sales managers develop high performing teams":

> Being productive means taking action on what matters most. You procrastinate when you know what you need to do but aren't inspired enough to take action or aren't disciplined enough to do the work that is necessary.

> (Iannarino 2015)

Ouch! That's pretty harsh.

I happen to have a different perspective on productivity and procrastinating. We live in a world where producing is king, yet often, it's easier and more fulfilling to produce when we allow ourselves time to be fallow. I argue that worrying about constant production often blocks creativity. I'm not suggesting you wait until just before your deadline to frantically finish a project in an all-consuming frenzy of panic. That's not allowing for creative flow; it's just getting shit done. I plan my projects carefully so I can handle the emergency moments that inevitably occur without feeling completely defeated or overwhelmed. When I say give yourself permission to procrastinate, I am suggesting that any creative act benefits from not forcing it. And most acts have some element of creativity, including sales and business.

In addition, this element of creativity can spring from percolation. How many times does an idea or a solution come to you when you're trying to focus on something else or doing something mindless like taking a shower? In his book *The Originals* (2016), Adam Grant writes: "Procrastination may be the enemy of productivity, but it can be a resource for creativity" (95). Procrastination often benefits creativity by allowing you to think about something else for a while, thus letting ideas come to you without intentional focus. Creativity sparks in unexpected moments.

Choose Intentional Procrastination

Are you stuck on an idea or a project? Unable to find your way in? Do something else that requires your focus and stop thinking about the idea. Procrastinate on your own, or grab a member of your team and do some of the following:

Go for a walk or a hike and pay close attention to all your senses.

Color or paint, either in or outside the lines.

Do something physical, play games, get into the flow.

Do activities that allow your mind to drift like washing dishes or cleaning up.

I hope that you wander through these pages finding inspiration from the words, the images, the activities, the examples, the explorations, and the questions. Read it in order. Read it out of order. Doodle and write in the margins and white space. Take a break to procrastinate. Open to a random page and discover something new. Flip to the Appendix and choose an Inspired Action to explore.

The most important elements of this journey are for you to have fun, be open, allow yourself to make mistakes, face your emotions, and play with the possibilities of your creative source.

PART 2

AREN'T CREATIVITY AND PLAY A WASTE OF TIME?

CHAPTER 5
Creative Play Is Serious Work

"I always think that focusing on fun is being lazy." The woman who typed these words had just asked a question about how to get motivated in the face of debilitating physical challenges that are affecting her work and her ability to produce or write. The expert leading this online workshop about how writing can help you claim your voice in professional settings responded that sometimes we simply need to focus on joy and having fun—especially when faced with so many obstacles. Yet this woman, who was dealing with more challenges than most of us, struggles with an issue that is ingrained in the American psyche, and possibly the world's, to the detriment of us all: the idea that playfulness, creativity, or fun has nothing to do with work.

We've been taught that playing is childish and a waste of time. Imaginative play has always lived in the space of childhood, reserved for growing minds as they explore the world. As adults, we are told it's time to get serious, get to work, and make money.

Psychologist Lev Vygotsky, best known for his sociocultural theory of development, said, "[. . .] a child's greatest achievements are possible in play, achievements that tomorrow will become her basic level of real action and morality." (Vygotsky 1978, 100). What changes between those early days of childhood and our adult world? We can talk about education, societal expectations, and so much more. Or we can think about the fact that young children play with possibilities and imagine themselves conquering whatever they can dream up. Nothing is impossible in a world of play.

Adults? Well, we focus on practicalities and realities. We have serious jobs to do. Fun and play are frivolous—reserved for only specific times and locations.

I've fallen into the trap of this belief system myself. After the publication of my second book, I found it difficult to write. The dry spell stemmed from a variety of things, including the fact that I was making such a small percentage off any sales of a book that took me months to write, after years of research. Meanwhile the academic publisher charged an arm and a leg for students to buy it. While I wasn't writing for the money, I became frustrated by a system that focuses on production without acknowledging labor or the needs of audiences.

I was also frustrated with my other worlds—theater and academia—where women's voices and the voices of minorities still struggle to be heard. I found myself thinking: *There is no purpose for my words or my art. There's no reason for me to write or create. Everything I do is useless.* I stopped blogging except for the occasional rant about the complex politics of our times. I journaled occasionally but couldn't maintain a consistent practice. I wrote specific project-oriented things, like theater programs and publicity for shows. But nothing stuck. Nothing made me move forward in ways that fueled my soul. I felt like a failure because I was not producing enough. As I've already mentioned, the pressure to produce often stifles the ability to create.

At the same time, I was still teaching in theater classrooms, so my creativity muscles continued to have some basic workouts. Enough to remind me that I had them. I had simply lost my inspiration, my spark, and my connection to the bigger reasons behind creativity and why it is so important.

The block began to shift as I worked with other people in a variety of circumstances. I wrote some of the stories, essays, and poems you will find in these pages in response to many inspired collaborative experiences, including workshops, write-ins, a devised night of theater, and online courses.

Rediscovering the intuitive tool of writing Morning Pages as described in Julia Cameron's foundational book on creativity, *The Artist's Way*, helped me reconnect with the flow and the surge of energy that unites us all. Learning to meditate led me to discover the innate connection we all have with a creative energetic source as well as with one another. All these acts built on each other, leading to another spark, another project, another connection, another story, another idea. With each new project, I rediscovered the spark of creativity.

By allowing myself to play and create with others, I had found my voice again. While doing that, I also learned one of my authentic truths—*life without creativity and the arts, without opportunities to collaborate and play with others, is a life without heart.* When we don't employ creativity and play with our inspiration, we lose confidence in our abilities, our own voice, and our capacity to produce quality work. As adults, it's crucial that we reclaim our right to creative play, that we understand the importance of creativity in everything we do, that we take the time to experiment and build our creative muscles.

CHAPTER 6

Collaboration Enhances Creativity

One of the most important ways we can begin to take creativity seriously is by creating collaboratively with other people. As mentioned above, the block I went through began to shift the more I worked with other people. A course I took about performance activism and the theories of Vygotsky led to questions of how to move forward without knowing where I was heading. The classes I taught in theatre for young audiences, applied theater, and a first year seminar called Creative Rebellion encouraged me to understand the how and why of performing with and for various communities. A challenging project between myself, a history professor, and courageous students reminded me how collaborative creativity can bring new understandings of who we have been historically and how that interacts with the stories we tell now.

With my new understanding of this belief, I realized that creativity is never a solo act. Books are a great example. They are a collaboration between authors, editors, illustrators, publishers, and—most importantly—readers. Without readers like you, who are looking for more creativity in your life, this book would never exist. Creativity, in its fullest sense, is always a conversation and a collaboration. In a world divided, we need more things that bring us together in healthy ways. I invite you to allow yourself to discover creative and playful outlets with a team of people who inspire you.

Build an Inspired Team

Ask your partner or some friends to create with you. Or join an online community that wants to create such as Spark Collaborative or the Global Play Brigade.

Count me in as part of your team! I love to get emails of your work. lisakramercreativity@gmail.com

Schedule time to create together.

Put it in your calendar and commit to it.

How to Find Collaborators

Perhaps you don't know who to invite to your inspired team. How do you find these people? As much as I believe creativity is for everyone, that does not mean we need to collaborate with everyone. It's both a necessity and a right to curate your community in a way that empowers collaboration and creativity rather than making things more difficult.

I find that working with certain types of people can both be draining and actually block access to the energetic pool of imagination that joins us. Some people like to put up roadblocks in the path of true exploration, which requires taking risks and being willing to fail. There are people unwilling to do either. Some people believe their talent is far superior to anyone else's, so they attack group members, rather than supporting them. Some people like to center everything around themselves and sow doubt in others to protect their place in the (nonexistent) hierarchy of creative worthiness. All these attitudes can truly affect collaborative groups by silencing some voices in favor of others. For these reasons, I am cautious about how I build my creative circle while still trying to provide opportunities for everyone to learn and grow.

However, when you develop a network of people willing to play and explore together (like your inspired team), it seems as if nothing is impossible. These people will:

- Listen with open hearts and minds.
- Ask questions and offer suggestions intended to help you improve or understand your work in ways that are kind and supportive.
- Be willing to play, explore, and be silly at times.

- Try new things, aware that sometimes things fail but that failure is something to celebrate and grow from.
- Be willing to commit to some kind of regular creative practice.

Here are some ways of discovering and building a wonderful creative community, if you are unsure where to start.

Live Workshops

Whether I am taking part as a leader or a participant in theater, writing, a visual art, or something completely different like learning about birds, I never fail to be inspired when working with a group of other interested people to create art, either collective or individual pieces. I find I am even more excited in workshops that invite people from across disciplines or opposing perspectives—creative approaches make communication across difference stronger. In almost every field, there are numerous conferences and workshops offered in a variety of settings, with a rich buffet of ways to explore ideas. Be courageous and sign up for one in your area of interest.

Another great aspect of live workshops is that they also help support local businesses. A local brewery in my area offers a communal space for workshops of all kinds. I learned to paint mini flowerpots at one and explored the power of arts for social justice at another. Independent coffee shops and bookstores often provide space for community gatherings or book club discussions. Public libraries often have spaces that can be used for a variety of events. Perhaps you have a workshop you want to offer; look for the places that will partner with you—not the corporate places but the locations and the people who will also become part of your local creative team. I can almost guarantee that if you have a crazy, creative idea you want to explore, you will find a group of people willing to do it with you.

Virtual Workshops

During the time of the COVID-19 lockdown, I discovered many powerful and playful ways to explore the world, even when we were separated by screens and distance. From laughter yoga to writing workshops, from storytelling to collage making, there are numerous virtual ways to reconnect with your creative self. The key to inspiration lies in the willingness of participants to try something new and the skill of facilitators to make everyone feel safe and inspired. Another advantage of virtual workshops is that participants can be from all over the world, thus expanding our connections with different types of people.

A simple search for workshops in your area of interest should lead you to any number of opportunities, some free and some with a fee. Seek virtual workshops where there is give-and-take, breakout rooms, and opportunities to create alone as well as collaboratively. Be courageous and share your work. The key to success is your own willingness to participate, ask questions, and take risks.

If you want to grow as a creative and playful person, I recommend joining a workshop focused on play presented by the Global Play Brigade (GPB). Full disclosure: I have participated in GPB offerings, led some sessions, and served in several of their planning boards, which also means I know exactly how beneficial they can be. The GPB was founded during the early days of COVID as a response to the separation and anxiety many of us were feeling. Here is a brief excerpt regarding their mission from their website:

We are artists/performers/therapists/educators who come out of the growing social movement of performance activism. We believe that integrating and utilizing play, improv, clown, theater and therapeutics into everyday life is a vital methodology for creating hope, possibility, emotional well-being and development.

(Global Play Brigade 2023)

As part of the Global Play Brigade, people from around the globe offer a rich variety of workshops, the majority of which are free. These are fun ways of connecting with other people and perhaps learning some new techniques to expand your own ability to see the world through new perspectives. Their emphasis on social justice serves as a reminder of the power of creative voices to make real change.

I also invite you to join me in one of my Gateless creativity/ writing workshops, where, as a certified Gateless Writing instructor, I use a unique approach to either writing or simply being creative in a fun, exploratory, safe, and supportive way. My workshops utilize a variety of techniques, including some from the improvisational theater world, like Yes, And . . . . I talk more about Gateless in Part 6, but I guarantee these workshops are worth experiencing. You can find them and other ways to work with me by joining the free online community called Spark Collaborative or reaching out to me through my website at lisaakramer.com.

Social Media

This one I list with caution. If you make the effort to actually have conversations via your favorite social media platform, respond to questions, and follow people who interact in some way, then social media can be a rich place to get your creative juices flowing. The danger lies in things like #writerslifts, which supposedly help writers gain readers but often end up being about one person gaining followers rather than building connections. There are also the risks that come from using platforms that don't protect their users from trolls or attacks. Creating and collaborating on social media can be draining if you don't take precautions. At the same time, social media offers an infinite number of ways in which collaboration is possible, as I will explore in Part 7.

There are many ways to build a creative community. Choose the ones that suit your needs, your goals, and your dreams. Then give yourself permission to create!

Find a Community for You

Explore ways to turn your solo creative acts into collaborative creative opportunities by joining groups, participating in write-ins, et cetera. Below is a list of places to consider looking.

Check your local library, museum, or arts center for workshops and groups.

Join Spark Collaborative, my home base for building a creative community.

Connect with the Global Play Brigade for free workshops that explore the intersection of play and social justice.

Sign up for an improvisation workshop, a place where creativity can grow.

Start your own writer's or artist's or creativity group for your community.

PART 3
WHAT IS CREATIVITY REALLY?

CHAPTER 7
The Science of Creativity

There are many scientific and psychological theories and explanations as to the source of imagination or creativity. These include:

- Material-realist theories that equate the mind to a machine. In these theories, creativity is invention based on existing ideas.

- Organismic theories that suggest phenomena like creativity must involve purpose and stress becoming and developing.

- Idealist theories that suggest creativity is a phenomenon of consciousness, and consciousness is the foundation of existence.

- Psychoanalytic theories that suggest the source of creativity is the same as that of neurosis and (in Jungian theory particularly) comes from the collective unconscious.[1]

I'm about to make a confession. I don't know which, if any, of these theories most align with my own understanding of creativity. Perhaps I see it as a combination of all things: a response to a given moment built on existing ideas, enhanced by consciousness, and present as part of our individual psychology.

Over recent years, as I learned more about quantum theory, that combination comes closest to my understanding of the source of inspiration. I prefer to think of imagination and creativity as being in the universe around us, in the energy that connects us, as living beings, with each other and with the earth. We simply need to tap into that energy in order to create.

In other words, believing in imagination and creativity is like having faith. I can't prove its existence with my own senses, although I can see and experience the results of creative actions in everything that surrounds me. It's even possible that creativity is not exclusive to human beings. Nature is creative. Animals are creative. A puffer fish designs complex patterns on the sea floor to attract a mate—instinct, for sure, but still an expressive act with a purpose. An octopus figures out a way to escape its confines, or a dog solves a problem to get what it wants. These examples define what creativity might be—problem-solving, expressive acts toward achieving something even if that achievement is simply the act itself.

Creative people look at the world, at a situation, at an unknown and ask, "What if?" "How about?" "Let's try." The imagination exists in a moment in time and place when we feel

---

1   For an explanation of these theories of creativity, I suggest reading "Creativity and the Quantum: A Unified Theory of Creativity" (Goswami 1996).

safe to explore these questions. It's a place where we let go and just see what happens, but that can only happen when we are comfortable enough to try or give ourselves permission to do so. That doesn't always happen in adult society.

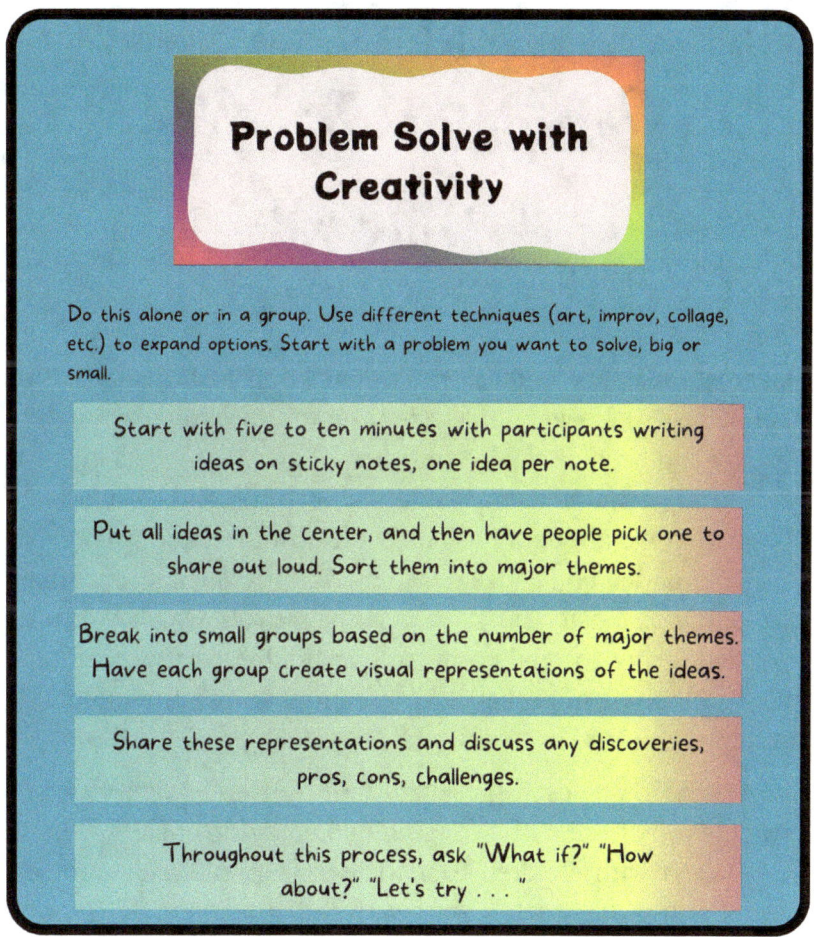

Problem Solve with Creativity

Do this alone or in a group. Use different techniques (art, improv, collage, etc.) to expand options. Start with a problem you want to solve, big or small.

Start with five to ten minutes with participants writing ideas on sticky notes, one idea per note.

Put all ideas in the center, and then have people pick one to share out loud. Sort them into major themes.

Break into small groups based on the number of major themes. Have each group create visual representations of the ideas.

Share these representations and discuss any discoveries, pros, cons, challenges.

Throughout this process, ask "What if?" "How about?" "Let's try . . ."

CHAPTER 8
Creativity Is Also a Muscle

Imagination is not faith alone. Imagination and creativity are also muscles. If we don't exercise muscles regularly, they atrophy and become flabby and weak. This is exacerbated if we feed ourselves mindlessly with empty calories and do not think about what we are doing to our bodies. In the same way, if we don't use our natural capacities to question, challenge, and think differently on a daily basis, we become weaker, which results in not challenging societal norms or questioning what we are told. We lose the potential that lives within us to ask the important questions that lead us to new discoveries.

At a TEDx-Tucson presentation in 2011, Dr. George Land presented the results of a longitudinal study on creative genius that started with children four to five years old and followed them through the years. They were all given simple tests to assess creative genius, which revealed the following:

- At four to five years old, 98 percent of the population qualifies as creative geniuses.

- At ten years old, 30 percent of the population can be considered creative geniuses.

- At fifteen years old, the number drops to 12 percent.

- In adulthood, the number drops again, all the way down to a disturbing 2 percent.

(Land 2011)

While this finding suggests that perhaps our approach to education might be hindering our creative ability, for me it also reinforces my belief in creativity as a muscle. When I was in elementary and junior high school, I took classes in gymnastics and could flip around the floor or the bars in ways that might surprise anyone who knows me today. Once I joined the swim team, though, I lost some of that flexibility and skill while enhancing other muscles. Now, even attempting a cartwheel would result in a lump of groans and laughter on the floor. I stopped using those muscles, so now they don't work as well. The same thing happens when you stop practicing a language or playing an instrument. Why should we expect our creative muscles to stay in shape once we've stopped using them regularly?

Discover Your Creative Muscles

Think back on things you loved to do as a child. What creative expressions and imaginative games filled your days? Choose one, and really think about it. Remember yourself doing an activity. Feel it. Smell it. Taste it. Then do it!

Draw a picture of your family, or friends, or yourself using crayons.

Get messy with finger paint or sidewalk chalk.

Play with Play Doh or clay.

Build a fort out of blankets, or a sculpture out of blocks.

Toward a New Definition of Creativity

If we think of creativity as both an energy of faith and a muscle that can be exercised and fed, then we discover that everybody has access to this important power and ability. Similarly, not everyone can have the "perfect" body or be strong in the same way. However, most of us have the capacity to be healthy, practice good habits, and make choices that improve our lives. Yet circumstances of life often make it challenging for individuals to choose things like play, creativity, or simply being in a moment of flow. When we are worried about where the next meal is coming from, how to pay bills, or how to keep our families safe, creativity becomes a lower priority. This is to our detriment because when we don't access our creativity, it can lead to depression, frustration, lack of joy, and even illness.

Of course, there are situations in which it may become more difficult for someone to exercise their creative muscles, often because of outside gatekeeping or societal decisions that limit access. For several years, a young man with severe disabilities attended a program I had created in one of my college classes. This program brought young adults from the public-school system's transition program (for people ages eighteen to twenty-two who couldn't graduate high school because of developmental delays) to work with my college students in creating a show for younger audiences. This particular young man was in a wheelchair, had limited movement, and could only communicate with the help of technology and his fabulous facial expressions. Yet he participated in every game and activity, contributed to every brainstorming session, and helped create every script. After a few battles with the system, we were able to borrow a more advanced technological device so he could even say lines he wrote himself, rather than being limited by the words and images that he usually had access to. His joy at being able to participate fully was evident and proved to me that creativity is a muscle *everyone* can use.

The challenges that come with social status, poverty, and other societal controls that people face daily make it more difficult for individuals to choose creativity. Yet, if given the opportunity, creativity can still blossom and grow within almost everybody. It's somewhat of a circular conundrum. Utilizing our creative muscles will enable us to find more just approaches to complex societal issues. However, if we are never given the choice or allowed access to our creative powers, we often don't believe they exist. We have the capacity to make wise choices, but we don't always have access to those choices.

Creativity does not have to be limited to available resources if we allow for a broader understanding of what it means to be creative. By this I mean creativity does not exist just in visual arts, theater, music, and dance. Creativity exists in everything we do. It underlies choices made in business, in health care, in government, and in almost every other field. Yet society, education, politics, and gatekeepers of all types often teach us differently. If we do not have role models who show us how to live creatively or are told that creative skills are not valuable or

CHAPTER 9

important, we often cannot choose to pursue our creative goals. Without voices of encouragement that say, "Yes, you can!" many people, particularly in lower income or minority environments, learn an unjust message: "Being creative is not for me; it won't get me anywhere."

But why won't it? This world has been built on imagination and creativity. Humankind has been creating since we began to think, to speak, to draw images, to tell stories so that people could find animals to hunt, or to explain the change of the seasons and create the myths of gods. Whoever discovered fire was creative. Whoever built the first shelter was creative. Whoever took an animal skin and said, "I'm cold; maybe I can put this on me to help me stay warm" was creative. Honestly, whoever looked at some of the grossest foods (like sea cucumbers—yuck) and decided to cook and eat them was creative.

It goes on and on. Whenever someone puts two disparate ideas or things together, they are using their imagination and developing something new or different. It may not always be original—ideas are always building on and borrowing from others—but the result is new for that moment, that situation, that person, and that question. As Austin Kleon says in the book *Steal Like an Artist*, "Every new idea is just a mashup or a remix of one or more previous ideas" (Kleon 2012, 9). Creativity lies in the space where that mash-up occurs.

By accepting this definition of creativity, you will discover the creativity within you. It's a matter of perspective. Are there ways you are being creative in your job or in your life? Are there ways you can make your work and responsibilities more fun, simply by shifting your approach? When you begin to see new possibilities in daily routines or approaches, you will then realize we all have something I call creative power.

CHAPTER 10
Defining Creative Power

Walk into any room where people are creating, and you can feel the energy buzzing around, no matter the form of work, the location, or the purpose. You can discover it in a meeting room at a conference where strangers or colleagues gather together for that moment, at that time, for that specific topic. They sit in groups to brainstorm ideas and find solutions to problems. You can hear and feel it in a theater classroom, where groups of performers rehearse scenes or improvise scenarios simultaneously in a cacophony of words, laughter, and occasionally overdramatized moments. You can almost taste it at a writer's retreat, where individuals spread out in cozy nooks and corners, drinking coffee, writing together in the collective pool of energy that surrounds them—inspired simply by the fact that other people are in the room writing as well.

While the act of creating and using your imagination is an individual process, the energy gained from creating with a collective only adds richness to your work. The location, purpose, scenario, and type of people can change, but the crackle of energy whizzing through the atmosphere always feels familiar. Inspirational. Powerful. These moments provide me with a sense of coming home connected to the world around me.

That is what I call the power of creativity.

This power does not belong to one group of people. Nor is it something we are taught, although it can be enhanced through practice and education. This power exists in us at birth. As children, we learn and discover things about the world around us. We play. We make mistakes. We try something different, something new to us. We discover.

I believe this innate ability is perhaps the most important power we have. When we access it, we find ways to make what seems impossible possible. When we explore through our creative lenses, we are able to question and challenge the world around us. This might explain why people who want power in a different way (power and control over others) often try to limit our access to creativity. If we make people only think in certain ways; memorize "facts" as dictated to them; and never allow them to question, to challenge, to try something new, or to mash new ideas together, we can control them. If we silence voices that have opposing opinions, then only one opinion becomes the norm. Whenever this happens, people are deprived of the natural ability to create, to question, and to think for themselves.

Unfortunately, we now live in a divided world. Among the thousands of other divisions, there is one in which people see themselves as either creative or not creative. Even those who see themselves as creative often divide the world between the serious moneymakers and the dreamers.

In this divided world, creativity is often seen as an aberration, meant only for those strange folks who paint or act or write or sing or perform any of thousands of creative actions that other people do. For many, creativity is frivolous, not for "important" real-world functions like making money or advocating for change or becoming "responsible" adults. We see it all the time when actors and famous musicians who are passionate about social or political causes use their platforms to make statements. Trolling comments follow in which they are told to "stay in their lane" or to shut up because they are just performers who don't know what they are talking about.

Creativity is seen as somehow disconnected from intelligence, real thought, responsibility, and adulthood.

In addition, creativity is often seen as an inherited gift that equals talent. When I taught a first-year seminar course called Creative Rebellion, I would ask my students if they considered themselves creative. I cannot count the number of times the answer has been something like "No, because I can't paint or draw or sing or act or play a musical instrument." Or "I think so, but I am not very good at painting or writing, et cetera." I like to think about things and wonder "What if?"

When did creativity come to mean that you had to be skilled at something? Skills like painting, drawing, playing a musical instrument, acting, et cetera can all be taught and practiced. True, some people are innately more talented at these things than others, but that does not mean they are more creative than others.

According to *The American Heritage Dictionary of the English Language*, the word *creative* means:

- Having the ability or power to create: Human beings are creative animals.

- Productive; creating.

- Characterized by originality and expressiveness; imaginative: creative writing.

- One who displays productive originality: the creatives in the advertising department.

Notice that none of these definitions contain the words "person who exhibits and is the best at specific talents or skills in a limited number of art forms." Yet, for some reason, this is how people think of creativity. Somewhere along the way, we are taught that being creative means having a specific productive talent, rather than seeing creativity as a way to look at the world around us and imagine new possibilities.

I want to be very clear; I believe creativity itself is a skill that can be practiced, developed, and learned. It is also innate — we are all creative beings. We are born with the ability to think imaginatively; to have new ideas; to question, challenge, and wonder. This is evident simply by the way we explore the world as babies and young children. As young people, we look at a stick, and it becomes a magic wand, a conductor's baton, a cane, a microphone, or even a gun. These are all acts of imagination and creativity. Or maybe we take a crayon and scribble stick figures and lines and circles and proudly hand it to our parents, saying, "Look at my beautiful drawing of our family." It gets hung in a place of pride on the refrigerator. This is a prime example of a creative act — unskilled, unpracticed, but truly imaginative.

Yet, at some point in each of our lives, possibly during school but also reinforced in our homes and by society, we are told that if you are not skilled, then you should not be creating. If you don't have talent, then you should focus on other things. If you can't do something to perfection, then you shouldn't do it. Perhaps the most complex message is this one: if it's not completely original, it's not creative.

These attitudes are problematic. I suggest we should look at creativity through some new lenses:

- Creativity is, and should be, the foundation of what it means to be human.

- Creativity is, and should be, the starting point for seeking solutions for the problems that plague us.

- Creativity is, and should be, a right of all human beings.

- Creativity is, and should be, the thing that unifies us all.

- Creativity is, and should be, the act of building on the ideas of others because originality is almost impossible.

- Creativity is, and should be, a power available to all.

Find Your Creative Superpower

Are you ready to discover your creative superpower? While you can do this alone, it is best with a team of collaborators, for a fun exploration into what's possible.

Make a list of the skills you use for work or in your life. What are your strengths?

Make a list of things you would love to change in the world or your work. Dream big.

Either in writing or discussion, explore how you use your skills combined with other people's to achieve the changes you seek.

Finally, have each person decide on a superhero name and pose for themselves.

Share without fear of judgment.

PART 4

WHY DO WE NEED CREATIVITY AND COLLABORATION?

CHAPTER 11

Creativity Is Collaboration, and Collaboration Is Power

"Groan! I hate group projects." I have heard that sentence hundreds of times. It's true. In school at least, group projects aren't always successful. There's often that one person who takes the lead and the one who skates by doing the minimum amount of work. Yet, in my classes, I always incorporated at least one group project. Often, in classes that weren't writing focused, the final itself would be a creative group project rather than an exam.

Why? Because I truly believe we need to learn how to collaborate better as a society. When we silo ourselves off and say, "I can do everything alone," projects suffer. Or worse, if we think, "I am smarter than everyone and don't need help," problems don't get solved, understanding doesn't develop, and nothing moves forward.

In an article titled "The Need for Cross-Sector Collaboration," Jeanine Becker and David B. Smith write:

The striking challenges of our time—such as health care, the environment, education, and poverty—are complex, whether on a local, national, or international scale. Yet all too often we approach these issues with piecemeal and even siloed solutions, and with efforts (however passionate, intense, and even exhausting) that aren't sufficient to address the problems at the scale at which they exist.

(Becker and Smith 2017, C2)

The challenge, of course, is how to get people to actually work together without trying to prioritize their part over the part of someone else. How can that be done?

That's where a touch of creativity comes in. In a way, creative approaches might be considered the lubricant that keeps all the parts functioning together. Or, to use another metaphor, creative approaches are a few of the important tools in a toolbox filled with different approaches to problem-solving. Without them, it's harder to achieve anything.

I'll turn for a moment to the tool of applied theater and improvisation to explain this more. A key principle of improvisation is to make your partner look good. This connects closely with the philosophy of Yes, And . . . but takes it a step further, as explained in the book *Applied Improvisation*: "Ultimately, when players are doing their best to make each other look good, all feel fully supported, and this creates a climate for collaborative creation and innovation" (Dudeck and McClure 2018, 282). If we apply this principle to the world of business, for example, it looks like supporting new ideas that might seem strange at first by working to make them better, rather than mocking or undermining the person who offered them. Making your partner look good is never about competition but, rather, about supporting one another. The key here is providing opportunities for all contributors to have buy-in on a project and to feel as if their contributions are valued and supported. That can't be done unless leaders utilize techniques that allow explorations, shared voices, shared stories, and opportunities to make mistakes without judgment. In other words, if we want more successful cross-sector collaborations, we need to bring in more creative approaches to collaborating.

In *The Artist's Way*, Julia Cameron offers tools for everyone to find the path to their own creative dreams and imaginative souls. In the introduction to the tenth anniversary edition, she begins with these words: "Art is a spiritual transaction." When explaining the basic principles of *The Artist's Way*, Cameron writes:

> If you think of the universe as a vast electrical sea in which you are immersed and from which you are formed, opening to your creativity changes you from something bobbing in that sea to a more fully functioning, more conscious, more cooperative part of that ecosystem.

(Cameron 2002, 1)

If we focus on the "ecosystem" of creativity, we are not bobbing alone in that electrical sea; we are bobbing together. We are simultaneously single entities and one with the whole universe of creative possibility. This is collective creativity.

Collective creativity is powerful because creative acts are always simultaneously individual and collaborative by the very nature of what it means to make art. Art of any form is a conversation between the artist(s), the subject, and the audience, even if that art remains in the pages of a journal. In that case, you become both artist and audience. Thus, creativity is a conversation and a collaboration. It is a form of call-and-response, action and reaction, communication and collaboration.

Imagine that you decide you want to build a sustainable house for yourself, but you know nothing about building houses. You don't have the right tools. You have a vision of what it should look like and how it will function, but you don't know how to translate that into reality. The initial creative idea comes from your spark, but you would never try to build it completely alone. Rather, you will share your dream with people who know how to design, to build, to create sustainable housing, to check the impact on the environment and any other issues that come up. As you develop the plans, there's give-and-take, questions, and challenges—always with that initial image in mind. As necessary, you add tools (which can be people) to the toolbox that will bring this project to fruition. In the end, the project is not exactly what you imagined but better. That's what happens when we work and create together. That collaboration gives you the power to achieve your dreams beyond your expectations. In this imagined case, it also becomes a powerful tool for change toward more sustainability.

What is more powerful than a conversation in which people come together, build on ideas, bring their individual toolboxes of skills and knowledge to the project, focus on the goals rather than one-upmanship, and find new solutions because they see things from differing perspectives? When we block off the possibilities of listening and responding (which are among the tenets of creative acts), very little gets accomplished. When collaborations are successful, we achieve more. The ability to work with others to achieve goals in new and interesting ways is the power of collaborative creativity.

Build Your Creative Toolbox

This is also fun as either a group or alone. You can do this as a drawing or actually get a toolbox and fill it with things that allow you to be creative.

Draw a tool box and write or draw inside of it all of the things that make you creative.

If you are using a real toolbox, use paint and stickers and markers to decorate it with your creative tools.

Make a list of things that can help you be creative (pen, paper, crayons, music, scents, paste, scissors, etc.)

If you are using a real toolbox, fill it with some of the tools you need, so you always know where to find them.

CHAPTER 12

Creativity Is Good for the Economy and the World

Imagine with me a world that focuses on creative economy. What would happen if we placed more value on artistic, creative, and culture-based thought and the people and ensembles doing this kind of work? According to the National Endowment for the Arts and the US Department of Commerce, the arts contribute more to the economy than do the construction, transportation and warehousing, travel and tourism, mining, utilities, and agriculture sectors (National Endowment for the Arts 2023). This suggests that investing more money in creative projects, products, and people can only help our economy and our communities by promoting change in interesting and sustainable ways.

Simply put, more money going into creative products and people produces more money coming out. Of course, I don't want a world where creativity and imagination always have a price tag. It's important to recognize, though, that a thriving creative economy allows for building and designing more infrastructure, developing better solutions for health care, creating jobs, investing in communities, and developing sustainable ways of growing. Creative approaches can enrich all fields and enhance the learning, growth, and innovation of most industries.

Individuals alone cannot develop a creative economy. We must work together across disciplines in a collaborative way to reach new goals and change how we approach what it means to be a part of the world. We need that to happen soon. The question isn't when do we begin but how. The answer lies in recognizing what has been missing in many people's lives, and that is a belief in and the practice of creativity.

CHAPTER 13
Creativity Enhances Skills

Several years ago, I had a young man participate in semester-long workshops who was on the autism spectrum. From the first day, Chris (age nineteen at the time he started working with me) would stare down his six-foot-something body toward his feet when I tried to talk with him. He wouldn't really respond to any questions. He participated in games physically but not vocally. By the end of that first semester, he took the stage with a roar (he was playing a lion in a show for young audiences) and said more excited words to me at the celebration after the show than I had ever heard from him before while looking me in the eye.

During his time working with me and other theater programs in the area, Chris gained confidence in communicating, listening, responding, and talking with passion. This enabled him to go to a job interview for a filing position in the courthouse. My partner in this project, Judy Freedman, went to the interview with him and shared the story of what happened. At the interview, at first, he wasn't talking much. Then Judy asked him a question about theater. From that point on, he had a lot to say. He got the job. He grew to become a confident presenter, has helped me lead one-day workshops, and tells his story with assurance and flair. Through creative explorations using theater games, writing, and other creative acts, participants learn to develop and enhance the so-called soft skills that allow them to thrive and grow in an ever more complicated world.

My friend Rachael Williamson, whose artwork appears later in this book, works with young people with learning disabilities and special needs. By encouraging her students to explore things in creative ways, she helps them discover their own voices. One of these students, Penelope, who has dyslexia, dysgraphia, ADHD, OCD, and anxiety, used poetry and art to embrace those as strengths rather than challenges. Rachael asked if I could include a piece of art made by Penelope. She wrote:

> I recently bought a "reverse coloring book" meaning that the colors are there, but you have to draw the lines/structure/layout of the art. My student created an AMAZING work today, and I think it's so fitting for your project.

(Williamson 2023)

When I saw the image, I knew she was right.

Jellyfish by Penelope Johnson (age 12)

I also knew I wanted to see if Penelope had anything else to share. I reached out to Rachael again, and she responded:

> Ooooooh. She wrote a poem called "My Name." She read her poem at a student of the month ceremony at the Woodinville Chamber of Commerce luncheon. She's the youngest student to ever win and her poem brought everyone to tears.
>
> (Williamson 2023)

After receiving permission from Penelope's mother, I am thrilled to be able to share Penelope's poem:

My Name

My name is from tough times
My name is from being bullied
My name is from being held back
My name is from what is wrong with me
My name is from learning I had dyslexia,
dysgraphia, ADHD, OCD, and anxiety
My name is from tears
My name is from I don't understand
My name is from needing help
My name is from love of animals
My name is from 2 schools
My name is from family
My name is from not giving up
My name is from exhaustion
My name is from pushing myself until I can't push
no more
My name is from grit

My name is from being kind
My name is from being a big sister
My name is from laughter
My name is from giving support
My name is from me
My name is from growing up but also not
My name is from color
My name is from life doesn't always go your way,
but you have to keep trying
Your name is your story because when somebody
says your name, they are just summing up your
story.
My name is Penelope Blythe Johnson

(Johnson 2023)

Why am I sharing these two stories? Because they exemplify what happens when you give a person permission to be creative, especially someone who's been told they are not "normal" or "good enough." It doesn't matter how old the person is. When they are allowed to explore the world through the lens of creativity, they often find their voices in powerful ways. Chris developed leaderships skills, learned how to be flexible (he was able to quickly problem solve when something broke on the stage), and discovered his passion. I haven't talked with Penelope, but her poem speaks for itself about her ability to grow beyond her "disabilities" and find the grit to keep moving. I think both their futures are bright, if they are allowed to continue creative explorations. Chris's story teaches us that, with practice, even the most reluctant or resistant participant can enhance the skills they need to succeed and lead. Penelope's story reveals that encouragement and support can enable us all to learn and grow.

Creative approaches teach these skills and many more that will be needed in the years to come. The world is changing, partially because of the pandemic but also because of technology, more concern for the environment, and approaches that are only serving the highest echelons of society. Work and leadership, as we have known them, need to change along with everything else. That's where creativity comes in.

Discover Your Creative Voice

Gather your inspired team together. Pick a topic or a question that you would like to explore. Prompts could be simple--a beautiful day, a time I laughed--or complex: What is my creative superpower? What does happiness mean to me? What does it mean to move?

Set a timer for ten, fifteen, or twenty minutes--whatever works for you and your inspired team.

Encourage everyone to explore the prompt using whatever medium they would like.

Writing, sketching, painting, video, sing, dance, collage, spoken word poetry--anything goes.

Come together to share without giving feedback.

Build on it: take the individual projects and merge them somehow. Then discuss.

The Skills We Need

Between the global pandemic, political unrest, and climate change, our world is going to need leaders and people with unique skill sets. According to Forbes, when we look just at business for example, these are the skills that will be in the most demand for at least ten years: digital literacy, data literacy, critical thinking, emotional intelligence, creativity, collaboration, flexibility, leadership skills, time management, curiosity, and continuous learning (Marr 2022).

Psst, I have a secret to tell you. These are skills that all of us need *now*, whether or not we are working in business. And they are all encompassed in some way by creativity—meaning you can strengthen the skills with creative approaches. Follow along as I explain.

Digital Literacy

Digital literacy is a technical skill and includes the ability to navigate technology and troubleshoot problems. Guess how some people learn to do these things. By playing video games, becoming content creators, and going down rabbit holes, which is a creative process.

Data Literacy

Data contains facts and numbers, or qualitative stories. The ability to extrapolate information from all that is called data literacy. While we would hope the reading is always honest, sometimes there are gaps in what is being studied. Sometimes the picture is blurred or manipulated to certain ends. Sometimes, as human beings, we interpret stories to promote specific concepts and ideas. Understanding the meaning of the numbers and telling a

story that less data-literate people can understand, involves—
you guessed it—creative thinking. Later, I will explore how
math itself is creative.

To explain how data literacy is creative, I turn to an article
called "Creative Data Literacy" by Catherine D'Ignazio, assis-
tant professor of civic media and data visualization at Emerson
College. She writes: "Data literacy includes the ability to read,
work with, analyze, and argue with data as part of a broader
process of inquiry into the world" (D'Ignazio 2017 7). She goes
on to discuss the fact that there is currently inequity when it
comes to data because "ownership of data is largely centralized,
mostly collected and stored by corporations and governments."
(D'Ignazio 2017, 6) Those without the technical knowledge to
interpret data often accept what is offered as fact without necessarily understanding the full story behind the data as presented,
including its limitations. D'Ignazio argues:

> [I]t is not enough to teach people how to read a chart,
> you must also teach them how to use that chart to
> make the world a fairer place. The practice of literacy
> is the practice of freedom, as conceived by [Paulo]
> Freire.

> (D'Ignazio 2017, 7)

Freire himself writes:

> It is as transforming and creative beings that humans,
> in their permanent relations with reality, produce
> not only material goods—tangible objects—but also
> social institutions, ideas and concepts. Through their

continuing praxis, men and women simultaneously create history and become historical-social beings.

(Freire 2000, 101)

Critical Thinking

Critical thinking asks you to question and analyze issues so you can come to conclusions based on evidence.

In other words, critical thinking encourages you to ask, "What if?" "How about?" and even "Let's try . . ." before you make decisions based on fallacies and misinformation. Revisit the inspired action Problem Solve with Creativity found in Chapter 7 to practice using these questions to develop more possibilities when faced with an issue. These are questions to inspire creativity and critical thinking.

Emotional Intelligence (EI)

In a blog post for the Harvard Business School online, Laura Landry, director of marketing and communication, writes: "Emotional intelligence is defined as the ability to understand and manage your own emotions, as well as recognize and influence the emotions of those around you" (Landry 2019). In my experience, there is no better way to strengthen your EI skills than exploring things from new perspectives and viewpoints: in other words, through creativity and improvisation. I have seen people overcome bullying by being given permission to create. I have also seen people who had nothing in common come together and become friends through creative processes.

Creativity and Collaboration

I hope you've begun to see how these two things are intricately intertwined. Creativity begets creativity and is always about collaboration, even if your only audience is yourself, because you are building on ideas that have come before.

Flexibility

In an article on the website WeWork, Steve Hogarty writes:

> Flexibility in the workplace means being able to quickly adapt to new circumstances as they arise. An employee who is flexible can change their plans to navigate or overcome unanticipated obstacles.

> (Hogarty 2021)

That sounds similar to the ability to Yes, And . . . doesn't it? Creativity demands flexibility. An idea rarely develops exactly the way you expect it to, but the power of creating is that we learn to adapt to any surprises or obstacles. When there is no right way to create, something will always go differently than you expect. The more you create, the more you are able to flex and adapt.

Leadership Skills

Not every creative person is going to be a great leader. However, I believe the best leadership comes from those who keep an eye on the bigger picture while allowing space for exploration, process, ideas, experiments . . . and yes, even failure. These processes are part of a creative journey. Great leaders also respect other people's time and opinions. They listen, question, admit mistakes, and are not infallible. All this can be learned and practiced through creative exploration.

Time Management

When a deadline is looming and the show must go on, the article must be submitted, or the painting must be hung, sometimes you have to come up with truly creative approaches to get the work done. Yes, the crunch can sometimes inhibit you, and creativity blossoms more when you are in flow. Still, that doesn't mean creative people cannot manage time. They just find creative ways to do it.

Curiosity and Continuous Learning

Creativity demands that you approach the world with curious eyes and a willingness to discover new things. Curiosity leads to new ideas and new possibilities. Learning asks us to question and explore. These are simply part of what it means to be creative.

When we look at things this way, the most important skills we can develop to help our world and design a better future for all are creativity and collaboration.

Examine Your Skills

Perhaps you are unsure how creativity fits into your own world. Perhaps you are nervous about how you can strengthen the necessary skills to stand out in the work force. Here are some ways to play with your concerns.

Take a skills test like Gallup Clifton strengths or Via Character strengths.

Make a visual image (drawing, collage, painting, etc.) of your top five strengths. Keep it where you can see it.

Explore the strengths you want to develop in timed writing or improvised scenes with a group.

Reflect with your inspired team on what you have discovered.

PART 5

WHO IS CREATIVE?

CHAPTER 14
A Team of Creative Geniuses

Creative genius is often depicted as one of individuality and loneliness. Picture the writer, cigarette dangling from his mouth, bottles of alcohol scattered around his room, as he frantically types words that represent the lifeblood pouring from his brain. Or imagine the painter slapping his vision onto the canvas, surrounded by artworks that may never be discovered until his death. My use of masculine pronouns is intentional here. For too long, the value of creative products, success, and individual genius have been defined in terms of mostly white men. While the reality is that women, trans, BBIMP,[2] and other marginalized artists have all been present in creative fields throughout history. Even today, male voices (often white) tend to dominate when awards are given out for creative work, and literature is still divided by categories that separate women's fiction from general fiction. These distinctions are important to understand because

---

2   This acronym stands for Black, Brown, Indigenous, Melanated People, as found on https://www.urbandictionary.com/define.php?term=BBIMP

these attitudes reinforce the idea that creativity is exclusive to only certain people in society.

Everyone has access to creative genius, but many people feel silenced because of this image of success. During the pandemic, author Neil Gaiman tweeted a response to a writer who was doubting they had anything of value to offer the world:

> Nobody gets to bring to the world the things that you get to bring to the world. So, saying that there are enough writers out there, enough directors out there, enough people with points of view. Well, yeah, there are, but none of them are you. And none of those people are going to make the art that you are going to make. None of them are going to change people and change the world in the way that you could change it. So, if you believe somebody that says, "no, no, we've got enough of those," then all it means is that you are giving up your chance to change the world in the way that only you can change it.
>
> (Gaiman 2020)

Gaiman's statement reinforces my belief that each of us has a story to tell, through whatever medium we choose to share it. Each story changes people and the world in different ways— sometimes with huge impact, sometimes with less. The act of creating them connects us with one another in ways that promote change that reaches beyond the limits of every individual. Together, our individual creative acts fill the world with a team of creative geniuses.

The first time I taught Applied Theatre and Community Engagement, the class contained a truly diverse group of students—diverse in terms of race, gender, religion, sexual identity (I assume), age, and even major. Only three members of the class were visual and performing arts majors (with a focus on theater). The largest cohort came from criminal justice and the remainder from biology, sociology, psychology, history, communications, and business administration. While I believe there is a creative element to all these fields, my educated guess was many of these students signed up for the course to check off the arts requirement or one of the other general education requirements this class fulfilled. In addition, theater courses often have a reputation for being easy. Little did they know they would be thrown into an environment where they were asked to think on their feet, let go of their inhibitions, learn to explore with words and images, and use their minds in creative and perhaps uncomfortable ways. On the second day of the course, something amazing happened as I wrote about in a blog post after the class.

Creativity in a Theatre Classroom

> We stand on the stage in a circle, a classroom of near strangers. I ask for a volunteer to join me in the center, to pose as a tree. I instruct her to say "I am a tree." Then we add to the picture, with suggestions by her classmates: a bird followed by grass. This is the beginning of the I Am a Tree exercise.[3]

---

3   For a description of this and other excellent improvisation team-building exercises see *Applied Improvisation: Leading, Collaborating, and Creating beyond the Theatre* (Dudeck and McClure 2018).

I decided this group would benefit from it because I could tell after the first day of class two days earlier that I would have a few reluctant participants. The person who suggested the bird was one of them, and tried to deny he said it, but I encouraged him to enter the image anyway, and he survived.

The activity achieves its goals and more. We move from that innocent tree, through various scenes, to an innocent black man with arms raised in front of the police, to a woman being cheated on, to a child in foster care. I do not guide this movement, or these moments of creation. I do not motivate these specific social statements or issues. It comes from the group. It comes from a community that is building and willing to explore issues that concern them. It comes from the collective creative energy that is growing in that space and at that time. I am thrilled.

(Kramer 2015)

On that day, each student began to discover their own inner creative genius—the one they hid behind the walls of being "too cool" or "too adult" to play. I knew then we would have a successful semester. By the end of the course, every single student in that class contributed in unique, creative ways. It all started by allowing them to discover that they were already creative; they just needed to be reminded of it.

CHAPTER 15
Surprise! Everyone Is Creative

"Not me! I'm not creative." "I can't do this because I'm not creative." I've heard it said in many different ways.

Each time, I reply with "Everyone is creative," often to eye rolls and defensive arguments. As I explained above, everyone has the capacity to be creative. However, if people don't believe in their own creativity, they get in their own way. They push this imaginative or creative instinct deep inside themselves, locking it behind thick walls. There are many reasons this happens: insecurity, society, education, or a lingering idea that anything fun or playful (which applies to creative acts) is a waste of time.

When I say everyone is creative, I mean everyone. I know there are many people who refuse to believe in their own imaginative or creative ability. I will acknowledge that there are times when creativity isn't the best option. For example, when I go to a bank, I would prefer the tellers follow a linear procedure rather than a creative one. I do want a creative doctor who can see beyond the protocols and restrictions of a broken medical system to treat people as individuals. Regardless, that's about jobs, not people. The people doing the jobs are still creative.

When we push aside this important part of our natural skills, we harm ourselves. We need creative and playful outlets to help us enrich our lives, get through difficult times, connect with others, and problem solve toward a better future for everyone, not just ourselves.

Think about the examples that follow.

Scientists Are Creative

When a scientist asks why or how something exists or happens, without expectations of a specific answer, they are thinking creatively.

Scientists themselves are creative. Albert Einstein wrote:

> At times I feel certain I am right while not knowing the reason. When the [solar] eclipse of 1919 confirmed my intuition, I was not in the least surprised. In fact, I would have been astonished had it turned out otherwise. Imagination is more important than knowledge. For knowledge is limited, whereas imagination embraces the entire world, stimulating progress, giving birth to evolution. It is, strictly speaking, a real factor in scientific research.
>
> (Einstein 1931)

Einstein's argument emphasizes that imagination is important *in addition to* actual scientific research and knowledge. In many ways, he was practicing the philosophy of Yes, And . . . by building on his ideas and imagination to discover unknown truths. Creativity is the place where ideas and questions are born. Ideas come from looking at the world without limitations or inhibitions.

Those ideas then can be strengthened and reinforced by analysis, research, and evidence. When we apply the philosophy of Yes, And . . . to combine imagination with scientific research and evidence, we create or discover something new.

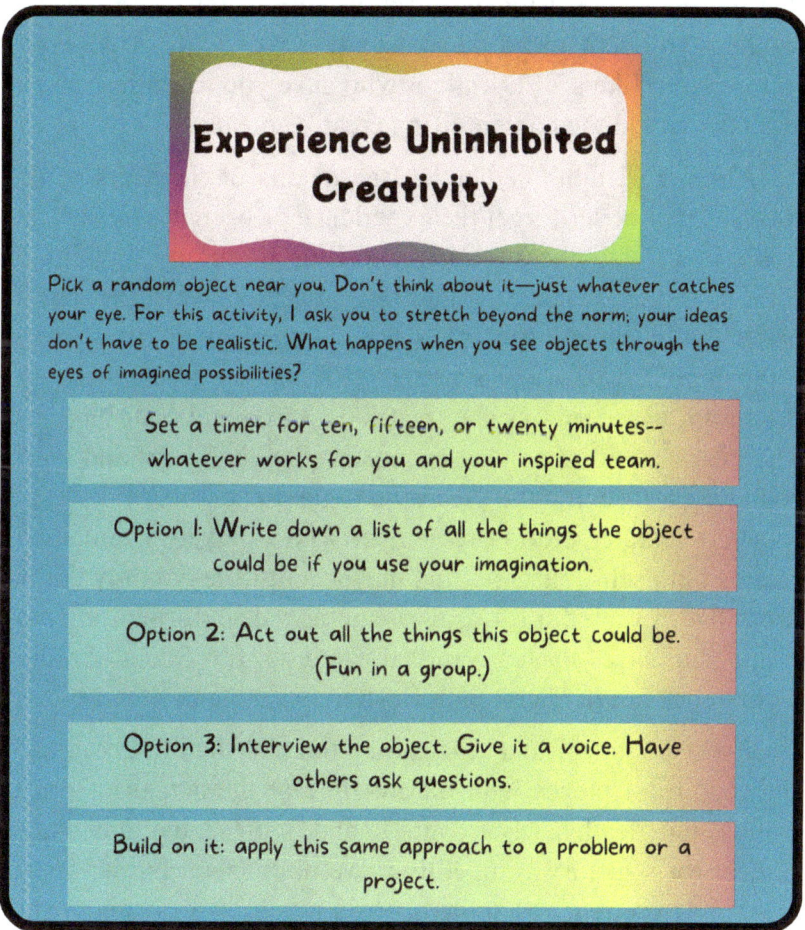

Experience Uninhibited Creativity

Pick a random object near you. Don't think about it—just whatever catches your eye. For this activity, I ask you to stretch beyond the norm; your ideas don't have to be realistic. What happens when you see objects through the eyes of imagined possibilities?

Set a timer for ten, fifteen, or twenty minutes-- whatever works for you and your inspired team.

Option I: Write down a list of all the things the object could be if you use your imagination.

Option 2: Act out all the things this object could be. (Fun in a group.)

Option 3: Interview the object. Give it a voice. Have others ask questions.

Build on it: apply this same approach to a problem or a project.

The Best Teachers Are Creative

We've all been in the classroom where the teacher stands behind a podium lecturing on a topic. You can tell they have given the same lecture many times before. Their voice drones in a way that motivates the listeners to fall asleep. Compare that to the teachers you remember the most—the ones who made every lecture seem like a TED Talk or who gave you activities to help you understand the content using creative means.

Although I don't remember the details of the Wars of the Roses, I will never forget the experience of bringing those wars to life in a living chess tournament. Rita Smith, my sophomore social studies teacher, found an amazing way for us to understand the characters, the story, and the complexity of these English civil wars. I collaborated with another student to write the script, based on our classmates' research and contributions. The members of a few classes took on the characters and made costumes to become the pieces on a giant chessboard. I wasn't a main character. I don't remember who I played. I remember feeling both self-conscious and maybe a little sexy in my purple dress that revealed a lot of cleavage as we performed in front of an audience at the National Counsel for Social Studies Conference at the Sheraton in Boston.

Every character had at least one line. We had to coordinate the capture of pieces with the timeline of the actual historical events and deaths. My coauthor and I presented the whole project for a history competition. We didn't win, but it was an amazing experience. I remember as much as I do about this project because of the creative teacher behind it. I think, in many ways, it has influenced my fascination with merging theater and history to this day.

Education that does not allow space for creative thought and exploration is ultimately education that fails our students. I saw it daily in my college classes, and I see it as I watch my daughter navigate through higher education. Nowadays, we all have easy access to "facts" (even made-up ones) with the click of a button and a quick search. We can find out dates and times and names. We don't need to memorize these anymore, and yet that is what the early years of education test. When students move on to college and are being challenged to think creatively and critically, sometimes they struggle. They struggle less if they have already been introduced to the possibilities provided by a creative teacher. Without that guidance, they often develop a "just give me facts; don't ask me to think" attitude toward learning. Rather than digging deeper to find the complexity of truth, they look for the easy arguments that support their biases and beliefs.

Mathematicians Are Creative

Math has rules. Numbers are specific. I've already mentioned that I prefer people who handle my money to follow the rules. Earlier, I suggested there are few rules to how we can practice creativity. However, it's interesting what happens to creativity when there are rules to follow. Rules can be aids to creativity rather than limitations. Following rules and then bringing in other ideas or possibilities is the essence of creativity. In many ways, the rules of mathematics are ones that have been created or defined to help organize our thoughts. Creativity is a dance between organized thoughts and new possibilities, which is why mathematics requires an element of creativity.

I am going to quote a mathematician on this:

> When people ask, often cynically, what *creativity* looks like, it is surely this: the ability to join seemingly disparate ideas to form new expressions of thought and emotion.
>
> By this definition, mathematics must be considered a creative pursuit. The mathematical world is governed by patterns and symmetries, some of them known and most of them awaiting our discovery.
>
> There are no topics in mathematics; only artificial barriers that we have erected to help organize the curriculum. At school, we study topics in discrete chunks and come to understand them as separate islands of knowledge. Yet the most powerful and interesting mathematics arises when we cut through these barriers.
>
> (Mubeen)

"I don't math," I often said when my daughter was struggling with homework. I still sometimes say it when I have to figure out the tip on a large, divided bill. Math challenges me much more than words. But, at the same time, math was the foundation of my designs when I considered becoming a lighting designer. Shapes and geometry guide my choices when I am staging a play. I recognize that the ability to turn the world into numbers and then turn those numbers into meaning of all kinds is, absolutely, an act of creativity. Math is the foundation of music, which for many is the epitome of a creative art form. Math also fuels visual art, providing a sense of symmetry and balance. Without math, our imaginative world would simply not be as rich. Therefore, mathematicians and those who use math in their work tap into a creative source guided by the rules and language of numbers.

People Who Work with Language Are Creative

My creative home lies between the worlds of language and theater. To me, the language of words (spoken and written) connects and intertwines with the language of symbol, of movement, of science, of music, of art, and of culture.

Words, to me, travel beyond the limited configuration of letters on a page. They are language to be expressed through voice, through song, onstage, and in story. To this day, I read everything I write out loud as a means of checking for flow, meaning, and mistakes.

I love nothing more than to hear people speak in different languages and wish I could learn every one by osmosis. As an adult, with the help of language learning apps, I have delved deeper into languages, adding in Japanese, French, and German and even attempting a little Ukrainian. I've explored the fascinating connection between language, culture, and imagination. Each language creates new understandings and images in my mind of the cultures from which it comes.

This suggests that anyone and everyone who uses language (including visual communication like sign language) is using creative powers. In an interesting video about thinking like a linguist, Dr. Catherine Anderson, a teaching professor in the department of linguistics and languages at McMaster University, explains:

Probably the most fundamental property of human language is **creativity**. When we say that human languages are creative, we don't just mean that you can use them to write beautiful poems and great works of literature.

When we say that human language is creative, we mean a couple of different things:
First, every language can express any possible concept. . . .

The other side of the creativity of language is even more interesting. Every language can generate an infinite number of possible new words and sentences.

(Anderson n.d.)

It seems natural, then, that I have created a life based on language, communication, writing, and theater. In many ways, theater is its own language. It contains within its essence a way of communicating across all boundaries. That communication has come to mean the most to me because I believe that through the power of story—or the power of creativity—we will find ways to work together toward a more just and connected world.

Play with Language

There are many ways to play with these prompts. Sometimes you might want to write or you may speak out loud. If you have diverse groups, I encourage you to incorporate all different kinds of language into your play.

Break into pairs and hold gibberish conversations with each other. It helps to choose a topic, but remember, no real words.

Have a conversation that rhymes, one sentence at a time.

Pick a simple word or topic like greetings and explore the many ways to say those words in different languages.

Create a story with your group, one word or one sentence at a time.

Have a conversation that can only be questions. A: "How are you?" B:"Why do you ask that?" et cetera.

PART 6

LEARNING TO TAKE CREATIVE RISKS

CHAPTER 16

The Pressure of (Not) Achieving

In his book *Taming Your Gremlin*, author and psychotherapist Rick Carson writes:

> Your gremlin is the narrator in your head. He has influenced you since you came into this world, and he accompanies you throughout your entire existence. He's with you when you wake up in the morning and when you go to sleep at night. He tells you who and how you are, and he defines and interprets your every experience. He wants you to accept his interpretations as reality, and his goal, from moment to moment, day to day, is to squelch the natural, vibrant you within.

(Carson 2009 3)

I see gremlins as a combination of inner and outer voices. No, I don't think there are a bunch of little creatures running around saying awful things to people. Rather, the voices of some of the people who interact with us on a daily basis merge with this inner narrator to make us doubt everything we do.

These voices can be especially loud when we choose an unusual path, like the concept of embracing creativity in a world that undervalues that particular skill. As soon as someone declares their creative dream as one of their main goals, the doubters and naysayers begin to speak. As soon as a writer says the words "I am a writer," questions are asked and pressure begins to build: Have you written anything I know? Are you making any money? How's the book coming? When will you finish it? Do you have an agent? Are you going to be the next J. K. Rowling?

While all these questions might be part of the dream, the truth is there are many paths to being a writer, both paid and unpaid. There are many ways to fulfillment with creativity. There are also many steps between deciding to write a book and sending it out into the world. These questions are the ones that come from a society that defines success in limited ways that can actually hinder the creative process, rather than supporting it. By this I mean a society that focuses on product alone.

This doesn't apply only to writing. As soon as a person says, "I want to make creativity a priority in my life," the anti-creativity gremlins (ACG) come out in force. This applies to actors, directors, artists, musicians, video game designers—pretty much anyone who dreams of a world where their imagination and playfulness take priority. It can also apply to everyone else, including people who push their creative impulses into a small container made of steel and concrete inside themselves. It's time to let those creative impulses out and to silence those gremlins. Amazing things happen when you silence the gremlins long enough for you to take creative risks.

Admittedly, these gremlins can be difficult to ignore. ACG whisper horrible "truths" that have the potential of immediately crushing these "unrealistic dreams." They say things like *Your path is doomed. You will fail. You have no talent. Nobody succeeds at that! You should do something practical.*

You might even begin to recognize some of those voices. They may start sounding like the other gremlins, the ones found outside ourselves. Real people—friends, family members, mentors—sometimes crush dreams in an instant, thinking they are being helpful and cautious because they care.

When the gremlins are at their loudest, I stare at blank pages or revise pages already written. I struggle to break through to the flow—the one that allows me unlimited access to words, thoughts, and images in a way that time passes. Flow means that hours later, I discover that I have actually achieved something. Perhaps I wrote a thousand words. Or maybe four thousand (on a really good day). Maybe I only wrote twenty good ones. As any writer knows, that can be a huge achievement.

But in a world where time is money and achievement is assessed only by finished products or dollar signs, small wins seem like nothing. The gremlins of failure say: *You still haven't solved the problem. You still cannot submit. You still do not have (a publisher, a contract, a backer . . . fill in the blank).*

Those gremlins are very noisy, very busy, and very pointed.

But I have good news! It is possible to defeat these gremlins or at least keep them locked away quietly for a while. There are ways to keep them silent or choose to learn from them. In the next sections, I will share with you some of the best techniques to silence the gremlins. But first, I will include a story of how I am dealing with my own because they will never completely disappear, and everyone struggles with their inner critics.

Finding My Muse-ic

I've always loved music, but I have never felt confident in my musical ability. I sang in a chorus for my synagogue as a child. I performed in musicals and theater camp shows, in which I occasionally got solos. I played flute and bassoon in my high school bands. Yet my fears stopped me from continuing as I grew older. Fears of never being good enough. Fears of making a fool of myself. Fears of failure.

Gremlins are loud! They aren't very musical either when their guttural voices speak in my head. *You aren't good enough. You aren't talented enough. Your voice sounds like a screeching cat. Give this dream up.*

YOU STINK!

I often write poems with the idea that they *might* make good songs. My thought process is something like *If I don't have the courage or skill to perform musically, maybe I can at least write songs.* Yet I have never taken the step of finding a collaborator to help me turn them into music.

Before my daughter was born, I took voice lessons, nurturing a long-time fantasy of singing jazz in a small cabaret or club, even if only for one night. My daughter is in college now, and that fantasy remains unfulfilled. I want more music in my life. When I have truly overcome the whispered voices of unforgiving gremlins, you will find me singing a song I wrote in collaboration with a composer while I recline on top of a piano in a small cabaret. I am determined.

True creative power comes when you take risks. While I haven't yet fulfilled my fantasy, I have ventured into overcoming my own fears of expressing myself with my voice. Below is a poem I wrote intentionally as an attempt at spoken word poetry. I recorded myself and uploaded it to my blog in 2015. Since then, I've gotten a little more confidence and connected with people who have more technical and musical skills. It took several years to go from the original to a more collaborative version. Several years of me finding and strengthening my own creative voice. Even as I type these words, the gremlins say: *Don't do it!*[4]

I Yearn for Music

I yearn for music
I wish I could reach inside my soul
and let the sound escape
fingers flicking over strings
or dancing over piano keys.
Black and white steps to
the secret inside of me.

---

4   You can find my enhanced spoken word version at lisaakramer.com.

My heart-song.
But I do not have the power.

I yearn to raise my voice in melody
perfect pitch climbing the skies
so that the heavens open up to joy,
or perhaps sultry, husky crooning
in the deep dark depths
of a jazz bar
as I fulfill a secret
bucket-list dream.
Long flowing gown moving with me
as I release my soulful sound.
But I do not have the courage.

My music is words.
Short, staccato, bursts of sound.
Tapping their way
into meaning.

Or perhaps the sibilant seduction
of syllables floating along with
meanings just beyond comprehension.
Can one sing with a pen?

Some days I envy those
who hold music in their palms
or whisper sweet melodies
through a gleaming instrument.
My instruments never really sang.

I yearn for music
the kind that carries you on
a wave of sound

whisking you away
to times unseen, worlds unknown
memories forgotten
deep inside your soul.

I yearn for the beat of a drum
ra-ta-ta-ta-ting along with my heart
teaching me the rhythm of the land
of hate, of anger, of passion
ba dum, ba dum, ba dum the truth.

I long for the whisper of a flute
enticing my butterfly-soul
to dance in the wind
colors flying the sweet truth
of my heart.

I desire the sultry saxophone
singing my soul deeper
into love
or sex
or romance.

I yearn for the power to sing my truth
in a language that goes beyond words.
A language that entices your body
into the sway
into the rhythm
dancing to the flow
galloping to the heart beat
of your very soul.
I yearn for music.

CHAPTER 17

Working around the Pressure to Achieve

What do we do when the pressure of the need to achieve blocks our ability to create? What do we do when accessing creative flow seems like an impossibility? What do we do when those darn ACG tell us it's a waste of time? What do we do when we lose hope?

I am about to offer you some techniques that really help. But first, I suggest you draw some pictures of your gremlins. Any of the gremlins. Draw a whole army of them if you need to. Then either tear them up into tiny little pieces or take them outside and burn them in a safe place.

Go ahead, do it. The book can wait.

Do you feel better? Great, now we can continue without their nasty comments whispering in your brain.

Alternatives to Critical Attacks

Unfortunately, we live in a world that thrives on attack and criticism. Vicious comments, brutal reviews, and negative interactions get more likes and attention than celebrations of good work and movement in positive directions. People often thrive on being difficult, challenging even innocent comments, or playing devil's advocate. While all this negativity might be fun and titillating for some, it actually makes it more challenging to create, explore, and make changes that benefit the world as a whole.

During an interview for a contract job working with thought leaders of all types, I was asked "How do you deal with difficult personalities?" In some ways, it feels like all we ever do lately is deal with difficult personalities. We live in an angry world. We've lost the ability (if we ever had it) to communicate across differences and disagreements because of entrenched beliefs that allow no room for discovering new ways of being and doing.

I don't subscribe to that. I am actively seeking ways to communicate better, to listen better, and to encourage some kind of neutral ground where we connect in a place where change can happen even if we don't fully understand one another. That's part of my vision for re-creating the world through collaborative creativity. That space of discovery lies where creativity and collaboration meet. It lies in a willingness to search for the good, the beauty, the things that work, rather than everything that is broken and ugly. It's a difficult thing to do at times, especially when you are dealing with difficult personalities, including those nasty gremlins.

I have been lucky, throughout my career, to learn from some of the best mentors who model ways of responding to work that I then incorporated into my own approach. I have this toolbox of methods I can dip into whether I am directing or teaching or coaching someone's creative work. Tools I adapt to meet the needs of specific situations, people, and individual goals. Just as there are no specific rules for collaborative creativity, I try to be flexible and always experiment with new ways to encourage people to grow.

One of my unofficial teachers is Liz Lerman, a choreographer, performer, and teacher known as the creator of the critical response process (CRP), which is a method of giving and receiving feedback on creative works in progress. The basic CRP method breaks down into these four steps:

1. Statements of Meaning: Responders state what was meaningful, evocative, interesting, exciting, striking in the work they have just witnessed.

2. Artist as Questioner: The artist asks questions about the work. After each question, the responders answer. Responders may express opinions if they are in direct response to the question asked and do not contain suggestions for changes.

3. Neutral Questions: Responders ask neutral questions about the work. The artist responds. Questions are neutral when they do not have an opinion couched in them. For example, if you are discussing the lighting of a scene, "Why was it so dark?" is not a neutral question. "What ideas guided your choices about lighting?" is.

4. Opinion Time: Responders state opinions, subject to permission from the artist. The usual form is "I have an opinion about _____, would you like to hear it?" The artist has the option to say no.

(Lerman 2023)

This approach allows for more generative conversations around creative work without raising too many hackles in the process. When teaching, directing, or giving feedback on productions, I always try to keep these steps in mind. I find that if my approach doesn't feel like an attack, people respond better and enhance their skills. Understanding the CRP process helped me codify my own practices.

During the early days of the pandemic, I became certified in another methodology called Gateless Writing. This method, created by author, editor, and "book shaman" Suzanne Kingsbury, is

> a methodology that uses creative brain science, ancient Zen, and highly-effective craft tools + resources to move you beyond the conditioned, critical mind to a place of limitless creative potential.

> (Kingsbury 2023)

What does that mean? Basically, Gateless recognizes that writing is not just a mental action but also a physical and somewhat spiritual one. It is connected with the fight or flight response innate to all of us. When we feel attacked, including by red marks scratched all over our work, we often either respond with anger (get defensive) or fear (shut down). Neither response is conducive to more creativity or even reasonable discussion.

Sadly, we have been raised to believe that criticism is the only way to learn and grow. It occurs everywhere. Red marks on school papers. Annual reviews. Critical analysis of books, plays, artwork, or political and social platforms. Some people thrive on this criticism, becoming more and more determined to prove everyone wrong. Many shrivel up and freeze, thinking, *If I can't do it right, if I can't be perfect, then I'm not good enough. I should just stop.*

There's the voice of those pesky gremlins again.

In a Gateless Writing salon, participants get out of their heads and out of their own way and simply write without fear of judgment. How does this work? Every certified Gateless instructor (myself included) approaches their salons a little differently. In general, though, there are five steps to a salon:

1. **Settling into the moment:** This can be done with meditation, music, or simply settling down and breathing as the group lets go of the day and focuses on the moment.

2. **Receiving a writing prompt:** These vary depending on the instructor, the group, the purpose, the mood, the weather. They can be questions, poems, words, songs, artwork, et cetera. Whatever the prompt is, it's always just a suggestion. Participants can write to it, write against it, turn it upside down, or completely ignore it.

3. **Writing:** The writing is always timed and limited. Sometimes it's short. Sometimes it's long. Sometimes there's music. Sometimes there's silence. Some people type; some people handwrite. The main thing is that participants keep their hands moving. If they get stuck, they are encouraged to focus on the senses and incorporate those. Or sometimes, a Gateless guide will offer a phrase for people to repeatedly write until they find their own way into the material. The focus is on the physical action of writing, rather than writing as a mental activity.

4. **Sharing out loud:** Everyone is invited to share by reading their work out loud. Nobody is forced to read, but once people become comfortable in this method, most of them want to read. Once the sharing begins, some important Gateless guidelines come into play.

5. **Receiving feedback:** Once an author has shared, they sit back and listen to people respond to everything that is working in their piece. This could be about phrases that sing, ideas that resonate, or moments that surprise or comments about characters, movement, structure, or craft. Nobody

offers suggestions or criticisms; they simply celebrate the things that work.

For those of you thinking, *this can't work. I need criticism to become better*, I hear you. Gateless works, though, because it provides a space of safety and comfort where people become willing to take risks. It works because participants hear excellent writing, learn to recognize the technique in other people's pieces, and begin to identify where their own work shines, as well as where it falters. It works because of the power of four basic guidelines:

- **Do not make disclaimers:** This means no explanations or excuses from the writer before receiving feedback. No statements of "I didn't have enough time," or "I'm not good at this." Without disclaimers, the audience focuses on the work as it speaks for itself.

- **Refer to the author, the narrator, the voice, the character:** When giving feedback in a Gateless way, we never mention the writer's name. Sounds crazy, doesn't it? But that gives the person psychological distance from the writing. The focus is on the piece, not the personality behind the piece.

- **Stay on the page:** We focus on the words and the story that is being told, rather than how it reminds us about "such-and-such a thing happening in *my* life." The focus is on the piece as it is written, not the egos and lives in the room. This too creates a sense of safety. We treat each piece as if it was fiction, even if we know it isn't, because the focus is the story and the words. This enables people to do incredible writing on personal topics without feeling judged for their lives.

- **Celebrate what's working:** The pieces that come out of a Gateless salon are first drafts. They are rarely, if ever, perfect. By focusing on what is working in any given piece, participants become intrigued to try new techniques, and begin understanding where their own writing might improve. They are not being attacked, but they are growing as writers.

The fun part of all this is the amazing variety that comes from any Gateless salon. One single prompt can result in fiction, essays, science fiction, poetry, rants, et cetera. The pieces can be humorous, sad, scary, or playful. They can be academic, romantic, spiritual, or geared for children.

Although I usually select my prompts based on whatever I am thinking about or something that inspires me that day, I sometimes leave it to fate by pulling a card from an oracle or tarot deck. These are fun because they are so open to interpretation, and the end results are always fascinating. For example, at a recent salon, my friend pulled the jasmine card from her Seed and Sickle oracle deck. The deck itself is described in this way:

> Each card carries two meanings; one for times when moving forward is important, and one to help cultivate your own well-being. Whether you are sowing seeds for your next big project or harvesting rewards for a period of rest, *The Seed and the Sickle* will accompany you on this journey.

> (Inkwright 2021)

The two readings for jasmine talk about not letting doubts and scorn get in your path and recognizing that "Jasmine always grows exactly where it means to, and so do you" (Inkwright 2021).

Following are three pieces written in response to the jasmine card. I set the timer for seven minutes for this prompt, which is not a lot of writing time, and yet the results were powerful and diverse.

The stars are my jasmine.
They are my refuge, my quiet.
Their sweet twinkling,
like a delicate scent,

makes me feel calm
and loved.
Like the flower, they
point in all directions,
as if to say,
"You are exactly where
you need to be,
and you can go
 in any direction
at any time.
Just choose one
and begin."

(Beckendorf 2023)

Jasmine is resiliency. In a tea, it is plunged into boiling water and produces an elixir that relaxes and calms the drinker. It's cozy but requires a test to be produced.

Boiling water is everywhere, and delicate blossoms still have a pungency that is unmistakable. You know the scent of jasmine. Its delicacy is its strength. As with other things, it can be mistaken for weakness, but jasmine only ever smells like jasmine. It can't be mistaken or mislabeled as something else.
When in doubt be like jasmine. Not for the nighttime flowering in the dark, but for the smell, the taste, the feeling so distinctive it can never be silenced.

(Briesacher 2023)

And my own piece from that session.

I plant my roots deeper into the earth, hoping to survive the storm that has been tossing me around for days, weeks, months, years.

Am I the tree that we planted in honor of our beloved dogs, the one that never grew? Its roots are now creating new life, new hope.

Am I the lilac bush that we planted last year, that is just about to open its dark purple flowers and gift us with its gorgeous smell? The sight of it outside my window makes me smile.

Or am I night blooming jasmine, a scent that comes
from memory, and carries the dreams of younger
me on its breath? Can I weather the storms and the
naysayers, the fears and the doubts, to blossom
where I am?

Can I grow even if it sometimes feels as if the world
is against me?

Only time will tell.

For now, I plant my roots deeper into the earth,
hoping to survive the storm.

These techniques apply to being in the world as well, not
simply focusing on creative acts. In her book *Unfollow Your
Passion*, fellow Gateless Writing instructor Terri Trespicio talks
about "how quickly and profoundly [the principles of Gateless]
can shift your mood and the way people respond to you." She
goes on to write:

> **Point out what's working.** For one full day . . . make
> it a point to call out, write out, point out, precisely
> why someone's work is brilliant. . . . This is about
> listening and paying close attention to what they're
> doing that's working, and specifically why. *Why* was
> that presentation strong? Why was that an excellent
> point to make? *What* did you notice about what
> someone said or did that was effective? Make a

practice of it and you'll find people opening up to you in new ways.

(Trespicio 2021, 226)

Of course, sometimes constructive criticism is necessary. We need professional editors to make our work shine. We might need specific practical advice in our jobs to fix problems. However, when we are in an exploratory creative process, criticism can get in the way. Often what holds us back from trying to incorporate more creativity into our lives, our relationships, and our work comes from a place of fear. We are afraid of doing things wrong. We are afraid of being embarrassed or scolded. We are afraid of our work or, worse, ourselves being seen as unworthy or a waste of time. Supportive approaches, as well as personal and collective creative challenges, can help us reduce that fear.

Become Gateless

The easiest way to learn how to be Gateless is to join a Gateless salon. I lead them through Spark Collaborative, and there are other opportunities around. Here are some ways to be Gateless with your inspired team or yourself.

Read Unfollow Your Passion, and use some of Terri's prompts.

Print out a piece of writing you have done. Highlight ideas or phrases that really work.

Listen to someone else read their work out loud. Make note of words, phrases, and ideas that speak to you.

Read your work out loud to someone else, asking them to make notes of what is working.

Do not ask questions, make suggestions, or criticize. Bask in what's working. Then set it aside.

CHAPTER 18

Follow Some Rules without Fear of Failure

Yes, I am actually saying that sometimes you should follow rules if you want to create with courage. There is no limit to creativity and the imagination. I also believe creative acts are often enhanced by limitations. I love writing prompts and prompts for improvisation in theater. I believe in setting time limits and guidelines. I believe in the importance of understanding rules of form, genre, and grammar before we bend, twist, flex, and explode them. I find that having rules and guidelines to follow can alleviate the stress to achieve or do things "right." When we focus on the act of meeting the guidelines, we often surpass them.

I am very much a "pantser" when it comes to writing. Well, I'm somewhere between writing by the seat of my pants and plotting and outlining a project to death. It depends on the project, and it depends on the point I am at in that project. In the early stages, I find an outline stifling, and yet I develop tons of lists. Outlining helps me later on when I discover the gaps in logic or world-building that need to be filled. Or, for a nonfiction project, as I write, I begin to better understand the path my readers will need to connect with whatever story I am trying to tell.

Actually, when I think about it, this is my approach to all creative projects. As a theater director, I always have a clear idea of what I would like my final production to be like in terms of concept, stage pictures, and beats or moments. I am meticulous about setting up a schedule for myself and my team. That way, we all know when I am working on specific scenes, when I want my cast off-book (with lines memorized), when I want to have finished blocking a scene or an act, when I will have a run-through, and when I expect my collaborators to have presented their ideas or finished their work.

The path to getting to the final production, for me, involves exploration, improvisation, trying and failing, collaboration, process, self-doubt, hopes of success, and everything in between. In other words, the process itself is about creative experimentation and flow around the more restraining structure of my rules and schedule. I try to make it organic so my cast discovers the specific images and moments I want to convey through their own exploratory processes. I welcome ideas from my designers and team that better my original thoughts because I don't claim to always know what's best.

To me, that is the whole point of working on a play. You can't beat the feeling when all the pieces from all the collaborators come together to surpass even your own imagination. Exploring with others enhances my ability to access creative thoughts and ideas. I am aided by collaborators and a deadline. I am also aided by the rules and expectations of the theatrical world. We rely on each other to achieve the end result in a timely fashion that is hopefully both entertaining and under budget.

What happens when we work on projects solo? What happens when all we have is a blank page, and the ideas are floating around our brains in a knotted mess that won't unwind? What happens when we don't have an actual deadline, but there are these vague expectations of achievement that surround us?

If you are writing a book, then it is expected you will finish that book at some point, especially if you commit hours and hours (and hours and hours) to getting the words on the page. *Otherwise, aren't you just being selfish?* that nasty little gremlin whispers with a cruel grin on his face.

People expect to see that book published quickly. The way publishing is often depicted in movies makes it seem like every author gets an advance, a book tour, and lots of publicity. And of course, authors have the money to live in gorgeous homes and escape to writing retreats in spectacular locations. Oh, and don't forget that every book will soon become a movie. The gremlins roll on the floor laughing. Unless people are familiar with the complexity of the publishing world, which becomes more and more confusing daily, these can be unrealistic expectations. Many new authors believe this and then give up in disappointment.

These questions and expectations come from those who subscribe to the belief that the only value of any given project comes when it is finished, paid for, and on display for all to see. But perhaps we need to embrace a different understanding of how creativity functions in order to truly understand its value to society and to individuals. What if the process of creating is more important than the product of creation? I believe that a good process most often results in a good product, even if it's not what was expected. Each process also teaches lessons that we can never predict.

What if a true act of creativity requires a letting go of knowing and understanding the end point? What if we allowed the rules of form and the expectations of experience to take us on a journey toward discovery without worrying about a deadline or the quality of a final product?

Many years ago, I took a series of workshops with two award-winning poets. While I've always loved poetry, I never studied how to write it beyond my high school classes and perhaps one class in college. These poets introduced us to a variety of forms and encouraged us to follow the rules for each form before we dove into our own creative process and style. Their lessons have stayed with me, and I still turn to them when I feel the call to play with words in new ways.

For some inexplicable reason, I became fascinated by the sestina, a difficult form of poetry that has a long history. The Academy of American Poets describes a sestina as "a complex, thirty-nine-line poem featuring the intricate repetition of end-words in six stanzas and an envoi" (Academy of American Poets n.d.).[5] Every once in a while, I dip my toe back into this form and publish the results on my blog, good or bad. What this has taught me is that when you follow the rules, you never know what can happen. Are my poems perfect? Doubtful. Sometimes they probably even fail. Failure is part of journey. We learn from our mistakes, and we grow as artists. When tapping into our powers of creativity, failure simply allows us to discover new approaches and try something different. It's an important step that shouldn't be avoided.

Below, I share a sestina that examines the possibility of not knowing anything and enjoying the journey anyway. I originally wrote this as a response to a course taught by psychologist Lois Holzman of the East-Side Institute called The End of Knowing, based on her book *The Overweight Brain* (Holzman 2018). This

---

5   The words that end each line of the first stanza follow a rotated, set pattern to be used as ending lines in the following stanzas. Visit https://poets.org/glossary/sestina for the specific pattern rules.

was a mind-bending course that dealt with complex ideas about collaboration, creativity, community building, and ways of knowing and being. I admit, at times I found myself completely lost in the depths of the discussions. To help me sort through my own confusion, I attempted this poem. The discussions in the course were always rambling and free form, shifting from idea to idea and from question to question. I often found myself wondering, *what are we even talking about?* I chose to write using the structure of the sestina, hoping I could make meaning of everything. The end result is a complicated piece that may not even read like a poem to some, but the structure allowed me the freedom to play with words and meaning.

A Sestina for Un-Knowing

I
In order to perform understanding, is it
necessary to give up knowing?
Knowing is a relationship between the person
(who "knows") and the object.
Can un-knowing be a different type of
relationship?
One based on acting, developing, and
performing understanding?
To achieve this, do we need to remove all
structure, through which exploring meaning
develops in the act of relating and connecting?
Or does developmental understanding come
when the tools of exploration are placed within
the support of structure?

II

Take this poem, a sestina, one of the most
complex forms in terms of structure.
Yet, this very structure allows meaning-making,
word play, and explorations without really
knowing
where the language will take you, or what
images might help make connections
between thoughts, people, culture, language,
and the object
of discussion. The very act of word-forming,
image exploration, and meaning-making brings
new understandings
where even if people disagree, the ability to
explore and question together will create
complex relationships.

III

A search for method, is all about developing
relationships.
The connections we make through playing,
exploring, arguing, discussing, loving, and even
hating, give our life stories the structure
through which we can rediscover and recognize
our journey as members of an ever-changing,
undefined, community where meaning lies in
developing new understandings
of the purpose and actions which make life so
complex and rich when you let go of the idea
that you know
all the answers to all the questions of what your
life is meant to be. I OBJECT
to the idea that all "facts" are debatable.
(That idea itself is leading humanity toward

self-destruction) but what if we EMBRACE the
power of possibility that comes by non-knowing
explorations, questions, and discoveries as we
develop connections?

IV
As we perform together through creative acts,
things that we can know (to the extent that they
are knowable) and things that we need not
know, we strengthen our connections
between ourselves, one another, our
environment, and the life-force-creative energy
that joins us all. The way to self-community-
world destruction lies in ignoring that creative
power, and not performing and practicing
relationships.
Our biggest threats and challenges to
performing beyond knowing lie in the objects
that hold so much power over the imaginations
of humanity—money, religion, traditional ideas
of education, technology, "Truth" or the idea of
"being right"—these are the structures
of a society that has lost its way assuming that
humans can be all-knowing.
Knowing "facts" (or claiming to know them)
is meaningless if we no longer seek answers,
question possibilities, or practice playing and
developing toward new understandings.

V
What is the purpose of seeking not knowledge,
but new understandings?

Is this just another attempt to define human life
as having greater meaning, or is it the search
for new methods of connecting?
With ourselves, with others, with our
environment, with our humanity, all without
truly knowing
what this exploration can bring, or where it will
lead? For the true power of a method-seeking-
meaning-making-story-building-life lies in the
relationship
between what we think we know, who we think
we are, and the un-knowable. The exploration
itself provides a structure
for communication, development, and action,
to which only the most stubborn "knowledge-
owners" can object.

VI
The struggle between the knowledge-owners
and the understanding-seekers leads to people
who object
to any idea, lifestyle, or life meaning that
contradicts an individual's own understanding.
We assign importance to our lives based off of
interpretations of learned "facts" (no matter
how close they are to Truth), which we then use
to structure
our choices, decisions, and lives. What would
happen if we used that structure for exploration
and connection?
or for challenging, meaning-making, and
developing relationships
between ourselves, our communities and our
world, without focusing on knowing?

ENVOI
The answers to these questions lie in developing
new methods and new structures for connecting.
They lie in being open to different
understandings and unexpected relationships.

Finally, they lie in shifting the objects of our
fascination from things and "Facts" to a world
of unknowing.

After I shared the poem with the other participants, people responded with their own creative works. Up until this point, most of the responses had been more academic. My friend Rachael Williamson (aka the teacher of the amazing Penelope Johnson) expressed her understanding in a painting. I then made a word cloud out of my poem and took her painting (with her permission, of course) to design two coasters, a hobby I was into at the time. In this way, ideas were built on each other in a conversation with no expectation of achievement or of final product. It was simply a journey into the unknown.

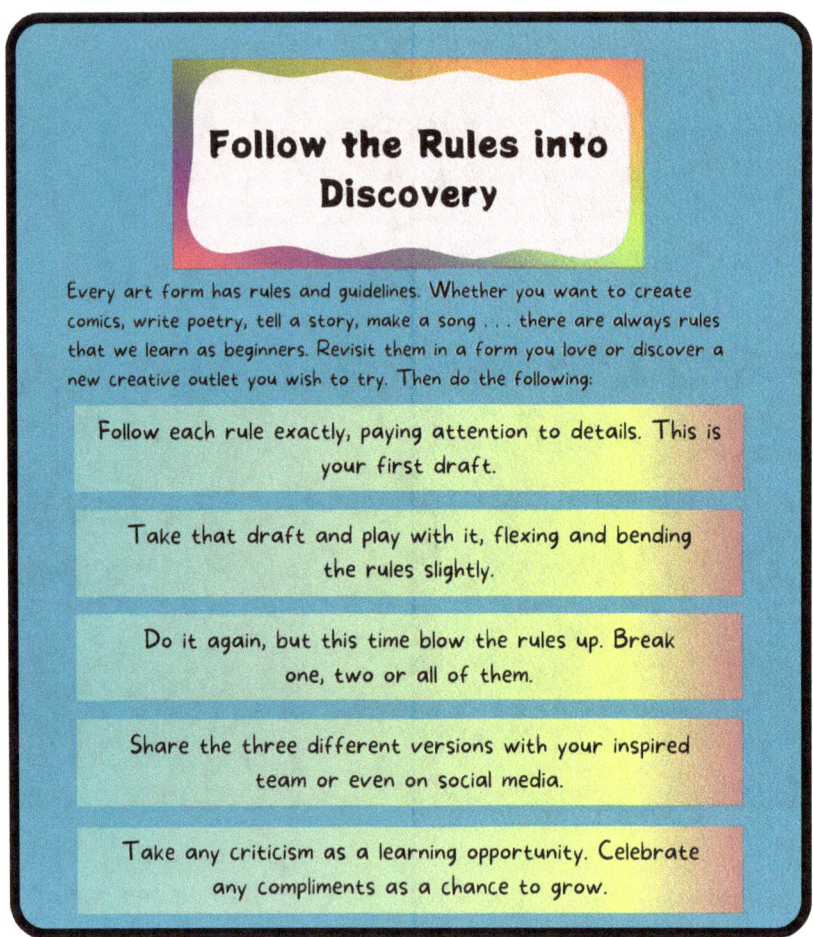

Follow the Rules into Discovery

Every art form has rules and guidelines. Whether you want to create comics, write poetry, tell a story, make a song . . . there are always rules that we learn as beginners. Revisit them in a form you love or discover a new creative outlet you wish to try. Then do the following:

Follow each rule exactly, paying attention to details. This is your first draft.

Take that draft and play with it, flexing and bending the rules slightly.

Do it again, but this time blow the rules up. Break one, two or all of them.

Share the three different versions with your inspired team or even on social media.

Take any criticism as a learning opportunity. Celebrate any compliments as a chance to grow.

CHAPTER 19

Flexing and Bending, Not Breaking

Sometimes I think the complex attitudes toward creativity come from a fear that creativity is all about breaking rules. Creative acts often seem chaotic or counter to the norms. This can be scary for those who want control, those who simply want unchallenged, quiet lives, or those who choose to see the world through the eyes of limited perspective.

People who embrace creativity often see beauty in what I call *creative chaos*. This chaos does not come from a desire to break all rules or destroy all norms. It's simply part of the exploratory process that creativity demands. Creative power enables us to reexamine the rules or norms established by society in ways that flex, bend, and sometimes break or change them to allow for more opportunities and ideas.

Creativity can be loud and abrasive, but it can also be gentle and quiet. Picture parents finding their own technique for potty training a child, after they've gone through all the expert opinions. Or a musician playing a gentle song in the background to create a romantic mood for a new couple. Creativity is also found in the flow of conversation among people, a flow that contains raucous laughter as well as whispered confidences.

The most imaginative people I know bend rules but don't break them without intention or careful planning. The most creative acts I have witnessed amaze because they understand the rules enough to bend them, flex them, and only on rare occasions intentionally break them in ways that make the world change. Every artistic medium has structures, rules, guidelines that help their audience understand and interpret the product. Actually, life is full of structures, rules, and guidelines. They are impossible to avoid. Some are stricter than others, but they all exist. For me, the most interesting people with creative power play with structures in ways that make them stretch into something new, different, and perhaps more inspired and more meaningful. Not louder and scarier, just different.

I believe structure exists in the moments (which are hopefully creative as well) between the flow of play and imagination. For example, some writers complain about the rules of grammar. "Why does grammar matter?" they ask. I am all for breaking those rules with precise intention, but it's important to understand them first. Masterful writers play with language purposefully, using the rules as tools through which they explore. They twist language in tantalizing ways. Play with fragments. With words. With sounds and syllables. Sometimes skilled authors create long meandering sentences that seem to go on in a rambling run-on sort of way but ultimately follow proper sentence structure; think Molly Bloom's soliloquy in James Joyce's novel *Ulysses,* which comprises a single sentence that contains 3,687 words (Joyce 1920). Not all writers are successful at this. The ones who complain the most are often the ones who can't be bothered to check or understand the rules of grammar. Or they relish rebellious creativity, which is a legitimate choice. They want to write the way they want to write. There's nothing wrong with that, but there is true beauty in intentionally crafting a sentence with an understanding of how language works, both in the written form and as a spoken tool that flows with its own musicality.

One word that repeats itself in these examples is *intention.* Intentional shifting of rules for a greater purpose is one of the most powerful tools of creativity. It is also one of the reasons I believe collaborative creativity is key to solving big problems in the world. People understand the rules of their area of expertise but not necessarily the rules of someone else's. When we develop cross-sector collaborations, these rules can run into conflict. As Kem Lowry from the Collaborative Leaders Network asks:

> How are conflicting knowledge claims, particularly those that pit "technical" and professional knowledge that comes from outside a community against "local" knowledge that comes from inside a community, to be acknowledged and addressed in ways that all participants will regard as legitimate?

> (Lowry n.d.)

Can you guess what my answer to Lowry's question would be? The intentional use of creative techniques helps people work through challenges and misunderstandings while finding ways to flex, bend, break, or work around the rules, which can lead to interesting solutions.

Many businesses have strict rules and protocols about how things should be done. Of course, when those rules and protocols have to do with safety, they *absolutely* should be followed. However, if those rules and protocols involve human-to-human interactions, then collaborators might benefit from a little flexible thinking or expanding beyond the confines of the rules—making the box of rules grow, stretch, and shift.

If your company involves sales of some sort and your team must follow a strict script to achieve their quota, what happens if that script does not work? Or if your company has strict rules about telecommuting, requiring certain numbers of hours of physical presence, what happens when a global pandemic strikes, and people realize they can work well or even better from home? The answers to these questions and so many more require the tools of creative thinking. Allow me to share an example from my life. I published the original version of this as "How to Lose a Passenger" just after my father passed away in 2012.

How to Lose a Passenger in One Phone Call '

I remember the day clearly. I had just returned from a successful presentation of a final class project for a college course called "Studies in Drama." The class, which consisted mostly of business and accounting majors, decided to create a piece of performance art and present it in the busiest location of the school. The students had the option to write traditional research papers individually, but instead chose the performative project, which they **thought** would be the easier choice. They learned, quickly, that creative options aren't necessarily easier. Their project required research, writing, preparation, rehearsal, and planning, creativity, communication, coordination, and perhaps a little empathy.

I came home excited about their success, only to receive the phone call I had been dreading. My father had passed away after a long decline with Alzheimer's or dementia. I collapsed onto my front steps, sobbing into the phone while talking with my mother. My husband jumped onto another phone calling the airline through which we had tickets for the next day to visit his family in Hawaii. He handed the phone to me, as I had to figure out the details for my flight. We decided it was best for my husband and daughter to travel ahead, as otherwise the entire trip would be cancelled, and we had not seen his family in a long time.

The poor agent on the receiving end of my distraught discussion had to stick to the script. That script included inflexibility of changing my flight without an exorbitant additional fee because my father had the AUDACITY to pass away less than 24 hours before our flight.

The only thing this poor agent could do was waive the $50 flight change fee, but that did nothing for the extra thousand or so dollars they wanted me to pay for a new flight a few days after the funeral (that's just one ticket, not for all three of us). They also refused to keep me on my return flight so I ended up flying alone, both directions, after laying my father to rest.

If the airline had responded with intentional responsiveness and flexibility and perhaps a little creative thinking, then everything could have been different. But instead, by sticking to a script that doesn't allow for empathy or human-to-human understanding, I have never flown this airline again. It used to be my go-to airline. Sure, they refunded me a pittance after I made a stink and wrote the public blog post, but it was far too little and far too late. This particular airline has a reputation of restrictive, inflexible, and unfriendly rules they refuse to bend.

Intentional. Responsive. Human-to-human actions that show empathy. Flexibility. Creative power challenges us to think outside the rules—not to break them but to bend them in response to changing circumstances and needs. These are all part of the toolbox that is creativity.

Wouldn't the world be better if we all learned how to use these tools?

Flex, Bend, and Break

Is there an area at your work or in your life that seems stuck? Work with your inspired team to explore new approaches to this challenge. The suggestions I make borrow from improvisation; however this could be done in writing or a visual art form as well.

First, lay out the rules as they exist. Create a physical representation with your bodies. Call out one of the rules.

Flex: What happens if you switch it slightly? Have the image shift and stretch. Change the statements to flex the rules.

Bend: This time bend your image. If people are standing have them bend over, et cetera. Can they still follow the rules?

Break: Blow up the image. Shift it completely. Ignore the rules.

Reflect with your Inspired Team on what you have discovered.

PART 7

COLLABORATIVE CREATIVE POWER IN ACTION

CHAPTER 20
A Tool for Connection

Creative power is a tool for community building, making connections, and discovering how to work across difference. It is an instrument that reaches beyond the individual toward a world that thrives on supporting one another across culture, social divisions, disciplines, and disagreements. I know this to be true because of my experiences teaching theater, writing, and other humanities-based topics to students of all ages, races, cultures, and social groups across the country and sometimes internationally. In Chapter 14, I described using the I Am a Tree exercise in my Applied Theater and Community Engagement class to reflect on what happens when you provide safe and comfortable opportunities for people to tap into their innate creativity. There was much more to learn from that experience.

The success on that day did not simply come from the reality that everyone is creative. That day was successful because I was not asking them to be individually creative. On the first day of class, they refused to perform a non-spoken story as individuals. Many of them were reluctant participants when I began introducing improvisational or playful activities that asked them to respond independently. Once I introduced the I

Am a Tree exercise on the second day, they worked together with other classmates to imagine, create, and inspire each other.

From that point forward, they borrowed from other people's stories, rather than having to tell their own in a public way. They dipped into the creative pool of shared experiences to make meaning and begin to understand each other in new ways. They even connected over a shared exploration into embarrassing moments. That day, and throughout the semester, they reflected on societal issues like justice and injustice, anger, relationships, et cetera. In one day, in one class, they felt the energy that comes from creating together, connecting with others, and the power of collective creativity.

In the book *Creative Collaborations through Inclusive Theatre and Community Based Learning*, I wrote:

> While I often teach students who are simply taking courses to fulfill arts requirements in a liberal arts curriculum, I . . . attempt to show them how their learning intersects with their lives, their communities, and their curriculum. Students in my classes are encouraged to bring their own interests and skills into their projects, thus connecting their science degrees with the physics of scenic design, or their business degrees with understanding theatre as a business.

> (Kramer and Fask 2017)

The students in that applied theater course were tasked with a final project in which they used the techniques and games they had learned in class to develop one-day workshops for one of four groups outside the college. The one activity every group included in their plans was I Am a Tree. The groups consisted of adult new immigrants, many of whom did not speak English; young adult new immigrants, many of whom did not speak English; and two groups of young adults with severe developmental challenges. This task required imagination, cooperation, a willingness to make mistakes and try new things, and an understanding that sometimes things don't work out and that they had to be ready to adapt. To me, those skills are important aspects of collaborative creativity. The key lessons from these public-facing classes were simple: when we let ourselves connect with our own creative genius and join that with the creativity of other people, incredible things can occur.

I have rarely experienced creative approaches failing to make a difference in people's lives and to at least begin to initiate changes in people's actions. Every experience is different, of course, as the cast of characters and performers changes, and the final goals shift, but ultimately, there is always a magical moment when creative power breathes life and possibility into any collaborative group. That's the power that comes through building connections across disciplines, utilizing the various talents within our groups and learning from and listening to the lived stories of all participants.

Connecting with Complex History

As another example, I share the following story of a more elaborate collaboration between the university and the community. On the evening of December 11, 2018, an eclectic group of people consisting of students, educators, family members, and community members gathered together at the Oaks, the historic home of loyalist Timothy Paine. The Worcester Timothy Bigelow chapter of the Daughters of the American Revolution (DAR) currently maintains this beautiful property as both a historic museum and the home of their chapter. The diverse group of people were all there to witness the end result of a unique collaborative educational experience: the performance of scenes researched, written, and developed by undergraduate and graduate students from a special topics course called Bringing History to Life team taught by Dr. Erika Briesacher of the history department at Worcester State University (WSU) and myself.

We went into that evening unsure of whether or not it would actually come together but proud of the work our students had done throughout the semester. We began the journey with an idea that theater and history (especially public history) overlap in that they are both rooted in story. When Erika and I first began discussing the project, she had already begun conversations with the DAR. I was a little hesitant at first because the group itself represents a historical tradition that is lineage based—and that lineage is (of course) predominantly white and Christian. However, we decided to encourage our students to focus on the stories that don't often get told, with results that varied from Irish maids to black servants to homeless people and even dipped a little into sexuality. The stories also ranged in time from the revolutionary period of the house to the Worcester Cold Storage and Warehouse fire in 1999.

One of the core questions asked in the field of applied theater is "How can theatre be harnessed in nontheatrical settings to build stronger communities?" (Taylor 2003). One of *my* core questions in the world of creativity is "How can creative approaches harnessed in noncreative settings help solve problems and build stronger communities across disciplines?" The National Council on Public History defines public history in this way:

> [P]ublic history describes the many and diverse ways
> in which history is put to work in the world. In this
> sense, it is history that is applied to real-world issues.
> In fact, applied history was a term used synonymously

and interchangeably with public history for a number
of years.

(National Council on Public History 2023)

If applied theater looks beyond theater and applied history looks
at bringing history to real-world issues, then this seemed like a
match made in heaven.

For these reasons, when Erika and I had the opportunity to marry
theater and history, we leaped. Both Erika and I value the power
of interdisciplinary learning and the possibilities that come when
we ask students to work beyond their comfort zones and their
disciplines in order to discover something new. We described the
premise of this course in our syllabus:

> This is not a history class *or* a theatre class; this is
> an integrated approach to understand **people's stories
> in historical context**. This is also a community-based
> learning opportunity with a local historical society
> and house museum. Students will conduct archival
> and historical research and construct narratives that
> will result in a theatrical performance, most often
> seen in living-history institutions.

Our hope for this course was to provide the students with an
experience that encouraged them to:

- Conduct research into primary sources and discover interesting stories of real people.

- Expand beyond traditional historical narra-
  tives to discover the stories and situations sometimes ignored.

- Learn how to tell these stories in interesting, accessible ways while staying true to historical "fact."

- Extrapolate from the historical evidence to understand the human stories found in the evidence.

- Discover ways of disseminating information beyond writing academic papers.

- Develop skills in collaboration by working with a group of diverse learners with differing skills and expertise.

- Encourage those who considered themselves artists to recognize the value of digging deeper into research and story while also encouraging those who defined themselves purely as researchers/academics to discover there is value in understanding their research through the lenses of empathy and creativity.

In some ways, that is a lot to ask of one course, but at the same time, all these things fall under one or both umbrellas of applied theater and public history. All these things are also skills that we need more of in the world. Thus, a collaboration like this had the potential to enrich learning on many levels for all collaborators and the audience.

The class was huge at around forty-seven people. This included students from across the colleges within Worcester State: different majors, different programs of studies, different cultural backgrounds, and different age groups. There was a definite divide between people who considered themselves artistic or creative (mostly the students who came from visual and performing arts, plus a few others) and those who would prefer to hide in the stacks of historical documents and only write academic papers. When we divided the class into groups, we made sure that each group contained a mixture of both. We made intentional choices to have people work across disciplines, often with strangers. Sometimes that led to tensions, but the truth is tension is possible in any collaborative project. The process of creative collaboration is not always easy or joyous—although we can experience laughter throughout—and it is definitely a challenge worth taking.

The end results were astonishing. Everyone's skills expanded. Everyone tried something new. Students accustomed to writing academic papers in a certain way or presenting information as a lecture of facts discovered there are ways to tell stories that allow for a little creativity while still remaining authentic to the research. Performers discovered that stories and characters are enhanced by delving deeper into the historical facts and details. Students crossed disciplines as well. The VPA students dug deep to find interesting stories in the archives and develop their characters. History students who swore from day one they would not get onstage took on leading roles in the performances. Perhaps most importantly, they learned how to collaborate. It was particularly exciting to watch groups made up of students from different generations and with diverse identities work smoothly together. One nontraditional student told us one of her favorite aspects of this course was that a "group of diverse students who had nothing in common came together and became friends."

The audience found the stories touching, sad, funny, interesting, and relevant to our own times. The women from the DAR realized they could bring more people into the historical home by providing creatively presented stories that stretch beyond its walls. Ultimately, this collaboration proved to me two arguments I have been making throughout this book:

1. Everyone is creative when they are encouraged to be creative and when they give themselves permission to expand their thinking.

2. Creative collaboration enriches projects, learning, and our understanding of what it means to be human. That understanding then extends out into the larger community.

Imagine what could happen by bringing people from science, humanities, health, and the arts together to solve some of the issues that face us today. Anything is possible.

Practice Collaborative Creativity

Every activity in this book can be turned into a collaborative one. However, if you want a few more ideas, here you go.

Tell a story together in which you go on a fantastical journey. A new person adds each new sentence.

Create a poem together, in which you are only allowed to see the line immediately before the one you write.

Start a collaborative art piece through the mail. Each contributor adds to the whole until the creation is done.

Pull out instruments and create a musical celebration that represents the day.

Work together to create a collage of your experiences.

CHAPTER 21

The Power of Sharing Stories

In the book *Creative Confidence*, Tom Kelley and David Kelley write:

> While unlocking our own individual creative potential generates positive impact on the world, some changes require a collective effort. You need teamwork—the right combination of leadership and grassroots activism—to achieve innovation at scale.

> (Kelley and Kelley 2013, 175)

Often the start of that teamwork begins with the sharing of stories as a part of team building toward collaboration. Teams can fail if people don't truly learn to listen to and trust one another. This trust is built through the stories we share.

When I use the word *story*, I don't mean only spoken stories, although those are important aspects of building collaborations. We all have stories and tell them in different ways for different audiences and situations. There is never a guarantee that the stories we share are heard or seen in the way we expect them to be.

There are no limits in how stories can be told. We tell stories through the tools of spoken or written language, theater, and music and dance or express them through the lines and colors of visual art. Stories can be found in political speeches or a simple note on a card. Music itself conveys stories that reach across distances and differences. Stories shared through multiple languages and multiple media lead to improved functioning and understanding in our complex world.

Chefs tell stories with their food. Home cooks do as well. Visual artists tell stories with their art. We find stories in the clothes we wear, how we decorate our homes, how we build our buildings, and the playlists of music we create. A garden can tell a story as much as a trash can. A shelter made of wood and found objects tells a story as much as a mansion. A protest tells a story as loudly as a political speech. If we expand our understanding of story, it allows for infinite opportunities to understand one another better and to perhaps write a better story together.

Stories are *always* collaborations and conversations between the storyteller and the audience, the interviewee and the interviewer, the craftsperson and the customer. They reveal who people are, what they believe in, what they hold dear in this world. Stories remind us of the things that connect us rather than divide us, as well as challenging the divisions that seem insurmountable. Stories show us what it means to be human. All that knowledge feeds into our ability to change the world, thus fueling us with true creative power.

We all experience stories through our own individual lenses, influenced by our experience in life. Each storyteller emphasizes certain aspects of a story to achieve certain goals. Each audience member responds to those elements from their own perspectives of the world. These are all imaginative acts that influence meaning and situations. The act of sharing a story has the power to build bridges or blow them up.

We can harness storytelling power to build more bridges by enhancing our storytelling muscles and learning to listen and understand better. The challenge in our society is that all stories don't get an equal chance to be shared. The loudest, wealthiest, most political, and sometimes angriest voices claim the focus. The people who have the money and the political power, or the "winners," control what and how stories are told. When they don't like the stories being told, they ban books, rewrite or ignore history, try to control what's taught in school, censor art they find offensive, and sometimes even silence democratically elected opponents.

Often people interrupt stories or talk over others, which is sometimes (not always) a power play that says, "*My* voice is more important than yours." In a patriarchal society, that often leads to men talking over the voices of women:

> Numerous studies have . . . reached the same conclusion: Men consistently interrupt women.
>
> For instance, one study analyzed 31 separate two-part conversations, 10 of which were between two men, 10 of which were between two women, and 11 of which were between a man and a woman. The researchers identified seven interruptions overall in the two same-sex groups combined; in the male-female groups, however, the researchers found 48 total interruptions—and 46 of them were instigated by the man. "There are definite and patterned ways in which the power and dominance enjoyed by men

in other contexts are exercised in their conversational interaction with women," the researchers wrote.

(Advisory Board 2023)

Gender isn't the only issue. There are also racial and cultural differences in how and when people interrupt. In recent days, interruption has become a politicized weapon to silence the voices of people someone doesn't want heard. For example, take this attack on a trans woman holding state office:

> Leaders in the GOP-controlled state Legislature on Monday continued denying Rep. Zooey Zephyr the chance to speak during proceedings . . . even after protesters chanted "Let Her Speak!" and forced them to adjourn temporarily.

(Hanson and Metz 2023)

When voices are talked over or stories are silenced, change does not happen. Collaboration stalls. Creativity stops. Listening and telling stories are among the crucial tools that live in the toolbox of collaborative creativity. Creative techniques will help participants share more productive stories, practice active listening, and learn to respond thoughtfully, rather than planning their response without actually listening to or learning from their collaborators.

Learning how to listen and understand stories is crucial to developing more collaborative, just, and democratic solutions to problems. Active listening makes all the difference, as explained below:

> Listening to others' **truths** helps us understand each other, so only when we begin to create the space for

these lived experiences to be heard can we begin to *understand* them and *learn* from them.

Ralph G. Nichols, a professor who studied the science of listening explained that "The most basic of all human needs is the need to understand and be understood" and that "the best way to understand people is to listen to them."

This is where "active listening" comes in. It's the practice of providing someone with your full attention when they speak, listening honestly and openly—**withholding judgement and opinion.**

(Waddington-Azambuja 2022)

It is possible for people to come together and make significant changes that help our world simply by developing stronger exchanges between speaker and listener, artist and viewer, writer and audience, storyteller and the world. When we practice collaborative creativity, we learn to listen to one another and build on what we hear. Collaborative creativity often helps us tell a greater story that incorporates the lessons learned by all involved.

Share Stories

A foundation of creative problem solving starts with sharing a story. This can be done in so many different ways. Try a few with your friends, your family, your inspired team, or maybe even strangers.

STEP 1: Separate into pairs, pick a topic, and have everyone share. Practice listening without interruption.

STEP 2: After both partners share, rotate pairs and tell the story you heard as if it was your own.

STEP 3: Repeat several rotations, always telling the story you just heard.

STEP 4: After several rotations choose one of the following options:

"Tell" the last story you heard with three movements OR create a visual representation.

CHAPTER 22

Collaborative Creativity in Response to Moments in Time

Simple moments of creativity and collaboration may seem minor, but they are often the beginning of bigger stories. Perhaps they strengthen friendships and memories, or perhaps they lead to global movements that change the world. Often these moments come because of an unexpected trigger, a devastating event, or even a moment of serendipity.

Starting with Serendipity

Some people define serendipity as a happy coincidence or "A combination of events which are not individually beneficial, but occurring together produce a good or wonderful outcome" (Wordnik n.d.). I suggest that serendipity is a combination of right moment, right time, right collaborators, curiosity, intuition, and a willingness to see possibilities even when things seem difficult or challenging. Serendipity is one of the tiny sparks that initiates creative acts:

[S]erendipity is not just a stroke of luck. It is
a reward given to one who dares to persist and
practice excellence in a chosen pathway. It is a gift
to one who rebels against all odds and is passionate
enough not to be limited in a quest by boundaries
or even logic and reason. It is an opportunity that
many let slip through fingers, but grasped by the few
sagacious enough to recognize it.

(Wimalasiri 2017)

Many years ago, my then-boyfriend (now husband) and I were living in southern Illinois. We decided to drive up to Chicago for a weekend and unexpectedly discovered that some dear friends from Hawaii were also going to be in town visiting family. Of course, we arranged to meet up with them.

That weekend just happened to include an event called Venetian Night, one of the longest-running summer festivals on Chicago's lakefront, where yacht and boat owners decorate their structures with lights and themes for a boat parade. Some of the famous tall ships were also touring the lake that year, so the spectacle would have been . . . well, spectacular. Unfortunately, the weather didn't cooperate. A deep, thick fog lay heavily over the lake, obscuring everything. A thunderstorm rolled in, and the four of us ended up huddled under an umbrella by the lake, eating Chinese food and trying unsuccessfully to avoid getting wet.

Sounds miserable, doesn't it? Actually, it was a wonderful, inspirational, freeing moment full of love and laughter. It remains high up in the ranks of my fondest memories. While we couldn't see the parade of boats, we witnessed a tall ship coming toward us out of the fog in a way that led to discussions of pirates and days of yore. (Those pirates again.) The sounds, smells, laughter, and spontaneity of eating together under an umbrella fashioned that moment in a serendipitous way to give us a perfect day.

That day, that event became the foundation of a mini collaboration. Later, after we dried off, we met again in a restaurant to eat some deep-dish pizza. After all, we were in Chicago. We couldn't stop talking about the perfection of the moment and the day—something we all experienced fully. We decided to create together by writing a poem. (Only two of us consider ourselves writers.) We grabbed a napkin, and one person wrote a line. The next person wrote a line in response, then folded the napkin down so the next person could only see the line immediately before theirs. This continued until we ran out of space. The results of that project can be seen here, both the words and the form they took when I incorporated them into a scrapbook about friendship and life.

Venetian Nights Chicago
(By Gerry, Cheryl, Nathan, and Lisa)

Spark on the mast
A gust of wind rolling the fog off the sea
A clipper ship setting off booming blasts
And lightning setting off ships' masts
Blanket drenched
Lightning strikes
Sparks fly
Why?
Buckingham spouts
Thunder roars
And the Chinese food tastes good
Under the blanket
Venetian Night
(Kawaoka, et al. 1997)

That moment in Chicago may not have changed the world, but when zillions of moments like this happen, the world changes. The moments can be small, like this perfectly imperfect day in

Chicago, or large, like the spark for a collaboration that has truly changed our world.

Creative Collaboration from Moments of Injustice

The more powerful moments of creative collaboration don't always come from sweet serendipity, but sometimes come from the tensions of current events. In recent years, we have been witnesses to and participants in incredibly powerful creative collaborative responses to all kinds of intense public events: from the outpouring of creative support during the pandemic to songs reacting to police brutality to student walkouts for climate change and the sharing of stories during the #MeToo movement that changed how we face gender relations. For example, the creation of another hashtag by three women in the wake of a horrible injustice started a movement that continues to change the world today:

> Founded in 2013 in the wake of the acquittal of Trayvon Martin's murderer by Patrisse Cullors, Alicia Garza, and Opal Tometi, Black Lives Matter Global Network is a chapter-based, member-led organization in the United States, the United Kingdom, and Canada, whose mission is to build local power to intervene in violence inflicted on Black communities by the state and vigilantes. We support the lives of the Black youth, families, queer and transgender communities, the disabled, the undocumented, those with records, women, men, and all Black lives along the gender spectrum. By combating and countering acts of violence, creating space for Black imagination and innovation, and centering Black joy, we are winning immediate improvements in our lives. From

pop culture to design to fine arts, artists inspired by #BlackLivesMatter understand that creativity transforms politics, transforms our individual relationships, and transforms the world.

(Black Lives Matter 2022)

The most powerful moments of creative collaboration live in the process and the journey toward expression, discovery, and change. There is no real endpoint or final product because every creative act, small exchange, monumental movement, or innovative action responds and reacts to moments fueled by serendipity and current events.

The power comes from the process of creating together.

Be Open to Serendipity

You cannot plan for serendipity. All you can do is be open and be present in life's moments. Here are some suggestions as to how you can use these surprise moments and messages from the universe as creative inspiration.

Carry a small notebook, a camera, or a voice recorder (or simply a phone) with you at all times.

When something draws your intention and gives you that flutter of "Wow!" make a note of it.

Keep these notes, images, recordings, and scraps of paper somewhere.

When you feel the itch to explore your creative genius, pull two-three out at random.

Don't select them; think of them as creative tarot cards.

CHAPTER 23

Creative Conversation and Collaboration in a Virtual World

In some ways, it has never been easier to collaborate and create with others. We live in a time when communication and interaction can happen at the speed of technology. Of course, when I began working on this book, we were limited by a distance of six feet, yet still, the ways of connecting were boundless. They became even greater as we moved out into the world again. More people work from home. More conferences and events are either fully virtual or provide virtual options, which enable access to more people. New social media apps are appearing. And more people are gaining access to technology thanks to some governmental programming.

Think about how different that is from the era when people had to write letters, which would take days, weeks, or even months before they reached a recipient or received a response. Artists couldn't post work in mere minutes. With the ease and accessibility of social networking and texting, we have more access than ever to collective creativity, if we use it wisely.

A Letter Is a Special Collaboration

I offer one side note here: writing letters is a fabulous and rewarding way of building a creative network. Sure, emails are much faster. Social media and texts can be almost instantaneous. But when you write a letter and send it to a reader, it allows so much more possibility. You can sketch pictures, ask and respond to questions, wax poetic. Simply choosing a card or stationery is a creative act. What happens if you include a picture or a dried flower or a card with a quote on it? How do you think, feel, respond, when you open a mailbox to find a letter waiting for you? These are all acts that strengthen the bonds of imagination and connection—the electrical ties of creativity between an artist and their audience. Writing and receiving letters is a dance of authenticity that strengthens relationships and inspires unexpected acts of creativity and collaboration. That, my friends, is creative power.

I recently had my own wonderful experience with the creativity involved in writing letters when an acquaintance on one of the newest social media platforms, Spoutible, put a call out for a simple gesture that supported the elders of the Pine Ridge Reservation. The Pine Ridge Reservation is an Oglala Lakota Indian reservation located mostly in South Dakota. According to the website True Sioux Hope Foundation:

> Pine Ridge Reservation serves as the home to more than 29,000 Lakota Sioux tribe members and is the poorest place in the nation. With 97 percent of the population living far below the U.S. federal poverty line, the living conditions on Pine Ridge Reservation are equivalent to those found among the poorest third world countries.

(True Sioux Hope Foundation 2022)

I knew nothing about those statistics when I saw this post on Spoutible. I just knew that a simple act of creative kindness could have a big impact:

> Please send a Yurok elder, some living in isolation on the far reaches of the reservation, a Mother's Day greeting card! These will be distributed by the Yurok Elders Nutrition Program with their once-a-week hot lunch delivery. It means so much to them to get a card. We started with Valentine's Day cards and they were an overwhelming success. They made such an impact.
>
> (Rojas 2023)

It was a delight to pick through my collection of hand-made greeting cards (made by others) to find a beautiful selection that might bring a smile to these women's faces. Just writing a short message and signing the cards made me feel connected to a world very different from mine and supported the creativity of both the card makers and the community.

Write Letters

Dust off that old address book of yours; get some stationary, a card, or a plain piece of paper. Pick up your favorite pen and write a letter to someone to whom you haven't spoken in a while. Be sure to ask lots of questions, but also tell your own interesting stories.

Spice this idea up by making it a collaborative project. Here's how:

Make it an art project that can only be finished by the other person.

Make a pop-up set design. Then send it to others for lights, props, and paint.

Turn it into a call and response poem or story.

The possibilities are endless with a few stamps.

Lessons Learned from Social Media

As much as I would love to return to the days of letter writing, it isn't very sustainable, and we do live in a virtual world. We can still harness the creative power of letter writing in these virtual environments if we come up with ways to work around the toxicity that often comes when people hide behind the anonymity of a screen.

I have a love/hate relationship with social media. I love the possibilities it represents:

- The ability to connect with people of diverse backgrounds and interests from all around the world.

- The ability to discover new ideas, explore amazing images and artwork, and support others in unexpected ways.

At the same time, I despise the dangers it can represent, including:

- The possibility of being attacked or doxed for a simple statement or for your identity, gender, or belief systems.

- The nauseating feeling that there is no real way to fight back against the above.

- The time suck: it's so easy to fall down rabbit holes.

As I work on this chapter, we are witnessing the downfall and destruction of Twitter, now called X, an app that for a while seemed to offer a solution that would enable everyone to share ideas. Unfortunately, it became a place of blue checks and non–blue checks and of algorithms that prioritized certain voices.

X is not alone in its toxicity, as abusive trolls and bots have hounded people, affected elections, and caused general chaos on many social media platforms over recent years. Yet there is hope because people have started to demand something better. In the hands of people who want to build a more collaborative world, the possibilities become endless.

As things became more toxic, I stopped spending much time on social media. I struggled with the unfortunate reality that it is both a place to connect and a necessary evil if you are trying to promote yourself or your work. I say "necessary evil" because we live in the world of late-stage capitalism where money talks, and the more money we have, the more we can do. Choosing to build a life around creative economy or any individual or collaborative venture is a challenge unless you have the funds to do it. I don't, so I had to learn how to promote myself in a world where I would rather be building legitimate connections. It's a fine and difficult balance. I much prefer promoting others and supporting their work whenever I can.

Things changed recently thanks to people like Christopher Bouzy, founder and CEO of Bot Sentinel, "a company specializing in identifying and understanding disinformation and targeted attacks on social media platforms" (Bouzy 2023). Upon realizing that changes brought by new management on Twitter would lead to even more aggressive behavior from people paying for blue checks, Bouzy reached out to his followers and asked if they would be interested in a new kind of platform, one that prioritized the safety of users from targeted harassment, threats of violence, and all types of hate. If he got enough interest, he would start creating it.

He received more than enough interest, and Spoutible was born. Bouzy asked for input from the Spoutible community from the beginning, including choosing the name and picking the initial logo. Building any social media platform requires a collaborative team, but Bouzy took the next step by incorporating the opinions and voices of the possible users. Each step of the way, he and his team sought insight from the users, including what capabilities people want to see in an app or on the platform. The platform continues to grow, adding new capabilities almost daily, in response to requests from users.

I added my name to the list early, but I took a while to officially sign up for Spoutible because of my aforementioned love/hate relationship with social media. I had a few doubts that there was any way to combat the ugliness that exists when we connect in a virtual world. When I finally decided to jump into the seas of Spoutible (Spoutible's logo is a whale, so ocean metaphors abound), I discovered a virtual home that feels like a completely different social media world. I'm not talking about the interface, which is similar to that of X, except better because of things like an edit button. At the time of this writing, Spoutible is still in early days, and there are occasional glitches. Those are minor issues compared to finding a space where people mostly feel safe to be themselves and interact in ways that are meaningful to them. For example, one spouter started a Spoutible banned book club. In her words:

> I am happy with the interest in banned books and the support for #SpoutibleBannedBookClub. When I initially proposed the club, I was taken aback by the enthusiasm, which is a good thing. Plus, the support for libraries and librarians is heartening.
>
> (Read a Banned Book 2023)

I found a place where people are supportive, friendly, interesting, and actually like to talk with one another. I discovered a place where people cocreate in long threads of jokes and faux "wars" over silly issues like whether cheesecake is a pie or a cake. (I am on team *piecaken*.) At the same time, your timeline can be filled with important news, issues, and calls for action. Every individual curates their own timeline to be what they want it to be because there is no algorithm but the users themselves. It's a place the users are building in a democratic and sometimes creative way. It is a virtual place of collaboration. Tensions happen, as it can in any collaborative atmosphere, but people also learn and grow from their mistakes.

Of course, the internet changes at the speed of technology. We never know who might be working on yet another social media platform. Christopher Bouzy and #TeamSpoutible have proven it is possible to create virtual spaces that are safe and inspire more creative collaborations. A platform like Spoutible or any others that are in process enables concerned world citizens to "make some noise and get in good trouble, necessary trouble" (Lewis 2022). It is possible for creative power and collaboration to grow stronger in a virtual world.

Learn to Make Good Trouble

The first step is to recognize that you are NOT the center of the universe.

Connect with a diverse network of people, either in real life or on social media.

Share ideas, ask questions, acknowledge that you don't know everything. And echo . . . echo . . . echo.

Take action on what you are learning, donate, vote, spread the word.

Access your CREATIVE POWER and use your voice, your art, your song, your intention without fear.

Work together to change the world.

PART 8

The Need for Collaborative Creativity

Conclusions: Bringing It All Together

In our world today, it sometimes seems like you take a risk just expressing yourself or suggesting that there might be better ways for us to all exist together. Being creative in a world of attacks can be a terrifying process, especially if you create alone.

In addition to divisions based on race, religion, gender, identity, et cetera, there seems to be another complex division:

- Only our way thinkers: People who view the world as one with specific rules and structures that must be followed. Any deviation feels like a threat.

- Creative thinkers: People who view the world through a prism that incorporates all colors and possibilities and allows for collaborative thought and change.

It's important to understand these two perspectives of the world. The first seems to thrive in societies that have strict rulers and followers. They want rules defined by someone way up in the hierarchy of human society. (God? Political leaders? Religious leaders? I'm unsure who.) Creative thinkers tend to be more open to finding new ways to work together so as to enable the voices of diversity and justice to play a bigger role in how we function as a larger human society.

While these divisions exist, I do not believe that it is impossible to heal the divide. Societal expectations, education, and access manipulate where people lie on a continuum between creative chaos and rigid structure. In order to change that, many systems need to change as well. It's a big job that begins with the spark of creativity and continues in a never-ending cycle of steps toward growth and change:

Step 1: Reconnect with your inner creative source.

Step 2: Build a space or a community where people feel safe to explore.

Step 3: Connect with others in creative ways.

Step 4: Share ideas and work through challenges.

Step 5: Build bigger and bigger collaborations.

Step 6: Make changes and share them with the world.

Step 7: Return to step 1 and repeat as necessary.

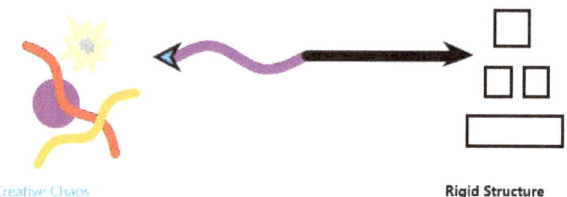

Creative Chaos   **Rigid Structure**

Creativity only thrives if treated as an ongoing process, one that continually changes, grows, discovers, uncovers. In addition, when it comes to creative works of any sort, they are intended to be a continuous conversation. Perhaps you read or watch something that sparks your own creative journey. You become part of an expanding conversation. Sometimes, as the conversation continues, minds change, and that's exciting. It's part of how we learn and grow as humans. The way we experience a creative act or product at one point of our lives may change completely when we revisit it later. The power of creativity is about embracing that change and saying it's okay.

The tools I offer throughout these pages are approaches that can help in any creative, collaborative, or innovative situation — even difficult ones. They can be used in complex discussions or to help develop collaborations across organizations. They can help in interactions with other people in which the risk of silencing voices stops progression or opposing sides can't even hear through their own entrenched opinions.

With every attempt at creativity, a person or a community develop their skills or learn new techniques. A writer plays with words in a different way or discovers a character who will appear in an as-yet-unthought-of story. A dancer finds the ability to move in a way they never expected. A musician uncovers a musical phrase or a line of poetry that sings them forward to their next completed song. A community creates opportunities for change that support all their members. A business community, using creative approaches, discovers a new solution to a difficult problem. A government, incorporating creative ideas, heals the broken parts of their society, one collaboration at a time.

Achievement does not just happen in a final product, as long as we redefine what it means to achieve. One step, one word, one creative thought, or one collaboration at a time is an achievement in itself. The best part comes when we share that achievement with others, when we work collaboratively. That is the true power and joy of collaborative creativity. It is also, I believe, our best hope for healing and re-creating the world.

ACKNOWLEDGMENTS

Throughout this book, I've argued that all creativity is collaborative. The truth of that statement lives in the book you hold, regardless of the form. The list of people who have helped this book come into reality is long. It includes every student who has ever played or created in my classrooms. It includes every collaborator who has ever worked with me on a project, and there are many. I am grateful to my group of Gateless writers, who have encouraged me with their own brave words.

But I would be remiss if I didn't express my deep gratitude for certain people who have helped this project come to life. First, I want to thank the team at Bublish, who pushed me toward the finish line, from cover design to enhancing the text in ways that made it stronger. I especially thank Shilah, my project manager, who was there for every question I asked and truly helped this book shine.

Special thanks to my collaborative partners and cheerleaders. Jessica Beckendorff, cofounder of Spark Collaborative, has helped me believe in myself and in what I have to offer. Rachel Wiese, cofounder of our theater company, Heart Forward, reminds me with each project of the power of collaborating with our community to create performance. Dr. Erika Briesacher, my cohort in collaboration and foolishness, reminds me every day what happens if we raise our creative voices against the establishment and the injustices in our society. My daughter, Sarah, and my husband, Nathan, are always there with love and support whenever I find myself doubting. My dogs, Yuki and Atticus, are also always there for comic relief when it is much needed. Also, thanks to Deirdre Assenza who took the time to read over parts of this book to help them make more sense. Thank you to Terri Trespicio, who helped me find what I really wanted to say through a workshop in which I wrote and presented a ten-minute talk.

Finally, of course, I want to thank those of you willing to explore the world through the lens of creativity: the readers, the dreamers, the creators, the artists, and everyone who seeks to find new ways of being and doing in this world.

Description of All Inspired Actions

(In alphabetical order)

Be Open to Serendipity

You cannot plan for serendipity. All you can do is be open and be present in all life's moments. Here are some suggestions as to how you can use these surprise moments and messages from the universe as creative inspiration.

- Carry a small notebook, a camera, or a voice recorder (or simply a phone with those capacities) with you at all times.

- When something draws your intention and gives you that flutter of "Wow!" make a note of it as soon as you can do it safely.

- Keep these notes, images, recordings, and scraps of paper somewhere—perhaps on your computer or filed in a drawer.

- When you feel the itch to explore your creative genius, pull two or three out at random.
- Don't select them; think of them as creative tarot cards.

Now create, incorporating all these moments!

Become Gateless

The easiest way to learn how to be Gateless is to join a Gateless salon. I lead them through Spark Collaborative, but there are many amazing offerings out there—some live and some virtual. If you can't, though, here are some suggestions for being Gateless with your inspired team or yourself.

- Read *Unfollow Your Passion* and use some of Terri's prompts.
- Listen to someone else read their work out loud. Make note of words, phrases, and ideas that speak to you.
- Read your work out loud to someone else, asking them to make notes of what is working.
- Do not ask questions, make suggestions, or criticize. Bask in what's working. Then set it aside for the future.

Build an Inspired Team

Ask your partner or some friends to create with you. Or join an online community that wants to create, such as Spark Collaborative or the Global Play Brigade.

- Schedule time to create together.
- Put it on your calendar and commit to it.

Build Your Creative Toolbox

This is also fun either in a group or alone. You can do this as a drawing or actually get a toolbox and fill it with things that allow you to be creative.

- Draw a toolbox and write or draw inside it all the things that make you creative.
- If you are using a real toolbox, use paint, stickers, and markers to decorate it with your creative tools.
- Make a list of things that can help you be creative (pen, paper, crayons, music, scents, paste, scissors, etc.).

If you are using a real toolbox, fill it with some of the tools you need so you always know where to find them.

Choose Intentional Procrastination

Are you stuck on an idea or a project? Unable to find your way in? Do something else that requires your focus and stop thinking about the idea. Grab a member of your team and do some of the following:

- Go for a walk or a hike and pay close attention to all your senses.
- Color or paint, either in or outside the lines.

- Do something physical, play games, get into the flow.
- Do activities that allow your mind to drift like washing dishes or cleaning up.

Discover Your Creative Muscles

Think back on things you loved to do as a child. What creative expressions and imaginative games filled your days? Choose one and really think about it. Remember yourself doing an activity. Feel it. Smell it. Taste it. Then do it!

- Draw a picture of your family or friends or yourself using crayons.
- Get messy with finger paint or sidewalk chalk.
- Play with Play-Doh or clay.
- Build a fort out of blankets or a sculpture out of blocks.

Discover Your Creative Voice

Gather your inspired team together and pick a topic or a question you would like to explore. Prompts can be simple—a beautiful day, a time I laughed—or complex: What is my creative superpower? What does happiness mean to me? What does it mean to move?

- Set a timer for ten, fifteen, or twenty minutes—whatever works for you and your inspired team.
- Encourage everyone to explore the prompt using whatever medium they would like.

- Writing, sketching, painting, video, song, dance, collage, spoken word poetry—anything goes.
- Come together to share without giving feedback.
- Build on it: take the individual projects and merge them somehow. Then discuss.

Examine Your Skills

Perhaps you are unsure how creativity fits into your own world. Perhaps you are nervous about how you can strengthen the necessary skills to stand out in the workforce. Here are some ways to play with your concerns.

- Take a skills test like Gallup Clifton strengths or Via Character strengths.
- Make a visual image (drawing, collage, painting, etc.) of your top five strengths. Keep it where you can see it.
- Explore the strengths you want to develop in timed writing or improvised scenes with a group.
- Reflect with your inspired team on what you have discovered.

Experience Uninhibited Creativity

Pick a random object near you. Don't think about it—just whatever catches your eye. For this activity, I ask you to stretch beyond the norm; your ideas don't have to be realistic. What happens when you see objects through the eyes of imagined possibilities?

- Set a timer for ten, fifteen, or twenty minutes—whatever works for you and your inspired team.

- Option 1: Write down a list of all the things the object could be if you use your imagination.

- Option 2: Act out all the things this object could be. (Fun in a group.)

- Option 3: Interview the object. Give it a voice. Have others ask questions.

- Build on it: Apply this same approach to a problem or a project.

Find a Community for You

Explore ways to turn your solo creative acts into collaborative creative opportunities by joining groups, participating in write-ins, et cetera. Below is a list of places to consider looking.

- Check your local library, museum, or arts center for workshops and groups.

- Join Spark Collaborative, my home base for building a creative community.

- Connect with the Global Play Brigade for free workshops that explore the intersection of play and social justice.

- Sign up for an improvisation workshop, a place where creativity can grow.

- Start your own writer's or artist's or creativity group for your community.

Find Your Courage

Is there a creative act you yearn for? Do your gremlins tell you no with loud and unpleasant voices? Let's silence them together. Repeat as often as necessary.

- Draw a picture of your gremlins and then crumple or tear it up. (Or burn it safely.)

- Be courageous! Follow your yearning and create something you have always dreamed of doing.

- When you are ready, share that creation with your inspired team or even on social media.

- If sharing is still a challenge, place it somewhere special; you'll know when the time is right for you.

Find Your Creative Superpower

Are you ready to discover your creative superpower? While you can do this alone, it is best with a team of collaborators for a fun exploration into what's possible.

- Make a list of the skills you use for work or in your life. What are your strengths?

- Make a list of things you would love to change in the world or your work. Dream big.

- Either in writing or discussion, explore how you use your skills combined with other people's skills to achieve the changes you seek.

- Finally, have each person decide on a superpower name and pose for themselves.

- Share without fear of judgment.

Flex, Bend, and Break

Is there an area at your work or in your life that seems stuck? Work with your inspired team to explore new approaches to this challenge. The suggestions I make borrow from improvisation; however, this could be done in writing or a visual art form as well.

- First, lay out the rules as they exist. Create a physical representation with your bodies. Call out one of the rules.

- Flex: What happens if you switch it slightly? Have the image shift and stretch. Change the statements to flex the rules.

- Bend: This time, bend your image. If people are standing, have them bend over, et cetera. Can they still follow the rules?

- Break: Blow up the image. Shift it completely. Ignore the rules.

- Reflect with your inspired team on what you have discovered.

Follow the Rules into Discovery

Every art form has rules and guidelines. Whether you want to create comics, write poetry, tell a story, make a song . . . there are always rules that we learn as beginners. Revisit them in a form you love or discover a new creative outlet you wish to try. Then do the following:

- Follow each rule exactly, paying attention to details. This is your first draft.

- Take that draft and play with it, flexing and bending the rules slightly.

- Do it again, but this time, blow the rules up. Break one, two, or all of them.

- Share the three different versions with your inspired team or even on social media.

- Take any criticism as a learning opportunity. Celebrate any compliments as a chance to grow.

Learn to Make Good Trouble

The first step is to recognize that you are not the center of the universe.

- Connect with a diverse network of people, either IRL or on Spoutible.

- Share ideas, ask questions, acknowledge that you don't know everything. And echo . . . echo . . . echo.

- Take action on what you are learning, donate, vote, spread the word.

- Access your creative power and use your voice, your art, your song, your intention without fear.

- Work together to change the world.

Play with Language

There are many ways to play with these prompts. Sometimes you might want to write, or you may speak out loud. If you have diverse groups, I encourage you to incorporate all different kinds of language into your play.

- Break into pairs and hold gibberish conversations with each other. It helps to choose a topic, but remember—no real words.

- Have a conversation that rhymes, one sentence at a time.

- Pick a simple word or topic like greetings and explore the many ways to say those words in different languages.

- Create a story with your group, one word or one sentence at a time.

- Have a conversation that can only be questions. A: "How are you?" B:" Why do you ask that?" et cetera.

Practice Collaborative Creativity

Every activity in this book can be turned into a collaborative one. However, if you want a few more ideas, here you go.

- Tell a story together in which you go on a fantastical journey. A new person adds each new sentence.

- Create a poem together, in which you are only allowed to see the line immediately before the one you write.

- Start a collaborative art piece through the mail. Each contributor adds to the whole until the creation is done.

- Pull out instruments and create a musical celebration that represents the day.
- Work together to create a collage of your experiences.

Problem-Solve with Creativity

Do this alone or in a group. Use different techniques (art, improv, collage, etc.) to expand options. Start with a problem you want to solve, big or small.

- Start with five or ten minutes with participants writing ideas on sticky notes, one idea per note.
- Put all ideas in the center and then have people pick one to share out loud. Sort them into major themes.
- Break into small groups based on the number of major themes. Have each group create visual representations of the ideas.
- Share these representations and discuss any discoveries, pros, cons, challenges.
- Throughout this process, ask "What if?" "How about?" "Let's try . . ."

Share Stories

Do this alone or in a group. Use different techniques (art, improv, collage, etc.) to expand options. Start with a problem you want to solve, big or small.

- Step 1: Separate into pairs, pick a topic, and have everyone share. Practice listening without interruption.

- Step 2: After both partners share, rotate pairs and tell the story you heard as if it was your own.
- Step 3: Repeat several rotations, always telling the story you just heard.
- Step 4: After several rotations, choose one of the following options:

  - "Tell" the last story you heard with three movements.
  - Create a visual representation.

Write Letters

Dust off that old address book of yours; get some stationery, a card, or a plain piece of paper. Pick up your favorite pen and write a letter to someone you haven't spoken to in a while. Be sure to ask lots of questions but also tell your own interesting stories.

- Spice this idea up by making it a collaborative project. Here's how:

  - Make it an art project that can only be finished by the other person.
  - Make a pop-up set design. Then send it to others for lights, props, and paint.
  - Turn it into a call-and-response poem or story.
  - The possibilities are endless with a few stamps.

WORKS CITED

Academy of American Poets. n.d. *Sestina*. Accessed 3 15, 2023. https://poets.org/glossary/sestina.

Advisory Board. 2023. "How often are women interrupted by men? Here's what the research says." *The Behavioral Health Crisis*. March 18. Accessed April 24, 2023. https://www.advisory.com/daily-briefing/2017/07/07/men-interrupting-women.

Amabile, Theresa M., and Mukti Khaire. 2008. ""Creativity and the Role of the Leader."." *Harvard Business Review*. October. Accessed February 17, 2021. https://hbr.org/2008/10/creativity-and-the-role-of-the-leader.

Anderson, Catherine. n.d. "Chapter 1: Thinking Like a Linguist." *Pressbooks: Essentials of Linguistics*. Accessed July 10, 2023. https://pressbooks.pub/essentialsoflinguistics/chapter/1-4-creativity-generativity/#.

Beckendorf, Jessica. 2023. "Jasmine doesn't grow hear." April 23.

Becker, Jeanine, and David B. Smith. 2017. "The Need for Cross-Sector Collaboration." *Stanford Social Innovation Review* 16 (1): C2–C3. Accessed April 22, 2023. https://doi.org/10.48558/8473-JD42.

Black Lives Matter. 2022. *Meet the Black Lives Matter Global Network Foundation's Growing Board of Directors.* April 27. Accessed April 25, 2023. https://blacklivesmatter.com/meet-the-black-lives-matter-global-network-foundations-growing-board-of-directors/.

Bouzy, Christopher. 2023. "Christopher Bouzy." *LinkedIn.* https://www.linkedin.com/in/christopherbouzy/.

Briesacher, Erika. 2023. "Something Tea." April 24.

Cameron, Julia. 2002. *The Artist's Way.* New York: Jeremy P. Tarcher/Putnam.

Carson, Rick 2009. *Taming Your Gremlin (Revised Edition): A Surprisingly Simple Method for Getting Out of Your Own Way.* New York: William Morrow Paperbacks.

n.d. "Creative." In *The American Heritage Dictionary of the English Language.*

D'Ignazio, Catherine. 2017. "Creative data literacy: Bridging the gap between the data-haves and data-have nots." *Information Design Journal* 23 (1): 6-18.

Dotigny, Eric. n.d. ""The Advantages of Positive Feedback"." *Small Business Chronicle.* https://smallbusiness.chron.com/deal-immature-employee-17590.html.

Dudeck, Theresa Robbins, and Caitlin McClure. 2018. *Applied Improvisation: Leading, Collaborating, and Creating Beyond the Theatre.* New York: Methuen/Drama.

Einstein, Albert. 1931. "Cosmic Religion: With Other Opinions and Aphorisms." 97.

Endocrine Society. 2023. *Endocrine Society*. https://www. endocrine.org/patient-engagement/endocrine-library/ hormones-and-endocrine-function/adrenal-hormones.

Field, Paul. 2020. April 17.

Foo, Sue. 2018. "2018-2019 2nd Provost Series Collaborative Teaching Grant." Worcester, MA, September 22.

Freire, Paula. 2000. *Pedagogy of the Oppressed, 30th Anniversary Edition*. 30th Anniversary Edition. Translated by Myra Bergman Ramos. Continuum .

Gaiman, Neil. 2020. April 21. https://twitter.com/neilhimself.

Global Play Brigade. 2023. *About Us*. https://www.globalplay-brigade.org/about-us.

Goswami, Ami. 1996. "Creativity and the Quantum: A Unified Theory of Creativity." *Creativity Research Journal* 9 (1): 47- 61.

Grant, Adam. 2016. *The Originals: How Non-Conformists Move the World*. Penguin.

Hanson, Amy Beth, and Sam Metz. 2023. "Montana transgender lawmaker silenced: What to know." *AP News*. April 25. Accessed April 25, 2023. https://apnews.com/ article/montana-trans-lawmaker-silenced-zooey-zephyr-d398d442537a595bf96d90be90862772.

Heilman, Kenneth & Nadeau, Stephen & Beversdorf, David. 2003. "Creative Innovation: Possible Brain Mechanisms." *Neurocase* 369-379.

History, National Council on Public. 2023. *About the Fields*. Accessed January 11, 2019. https://ncph.org/what-is-public-history/about-the-field/.

Hogarty, Steve. 2021. "What is Flexibility in the Workplace." *WeWork Ideas*. March 1. Accessed July 10, 2023. https://www.wework.com/ideas/professional-development/management-leadership/flexibility-in-the-workplace.

Holzman, Lois. 2018. *The Overweight Brain: How our obsession with knowing keeps us from getting smart enough to make a better world*. New York: East Side Institute Press.

Iannarino, Anthony. 2015. "10 Enemies of Productivity." *The Sales Blog*. February 10. Accessed April 27, 2023. https://www.thesalesblog.com/blog/10-enemies-productivity#.

Inkwright, Fez. 2021. "The Seed & Sickle Oracle Deck." Sterling Ethos.

Jeffries, Stuart. 2014. "How the web lost its way – and its founding principles." *The Guardian*. August 24. Accessed April 25, 2023.

Johnson, Penelope Blythe. 2023. "My Name."

Joyce, James. n.d. *Ulysses*.

Kawaoka, Gerry, Cheryl Treiber-Kawaoka, Nathan K. Lee, and Lisa A. Kramer. 1997. "Venetian Night's Chicago." Chicago, July 7.

Kelley, Tom, and David Kelley. 2013. *Creative Confidence: Unleashing the Creative Potential Within Us Al*. New York: Currency.

Kingsbury, Suzanne. n.d. *Suzanne Kingsbury*. https://suzannekingsbury.net/for-writers-only/gateless-writing/.

Kleon, Austin. 2012. *Steal Like an Artist: 10 Things Nobody Told You About Being Creative*. Workman Publishing .

Kramer, Lisa A. 2015. "Creativity in a Theatre Classroom." *lisaakramer.com*.

Kramer, Lisa A., and Judy Freedman Fask. 2017. *Creative Collaborations through Inclusive Theatre and Community Based Learning: Students in Transition*. New York: Palgrave Macmillan.

Land, George. 2011. "The Failure of Success." *TED-X*. Lecture. Tucson, February 16. https://youtu.be/ZfKMq-rYtnc.

Landry, Laura. 2019. *Why Emotional Intelligence is Important in Leadership*. April 03. Accessed 2023. https://online.hbs.edu/blog/post/emotional-intelligence-in-leadership#:.

Lerman, Liz. 2023. "Liz Lerman's Critical Response Process: The Basics." *Critical Response Process*. Accessed 2023. https://lizlerman.com/wp-content/uploads/2020/04/Critical-Response-Process-in-Brief_CRP-one-pager_updated-2020_03_24.pdf.

Lewis, John. 2022. "Get in Good Trouble." *Laidlaw Scholars*. February 21. https://laidlawscholars.network/posts/get-in-good-trouble.

Lowry, Kem. n.d. "Cross Sector Collabration Dilemmas and Tensions." *Collaborative Leaders Network*. Accessed April 23, 2023. https://collaborativeleadersnetwork.org/ideas/cross-sector-collaboration-dilemmas-and-tensions/.

Marr, Bernard. 2022. "The Top 10 Most In-Demand Skills For The Next 10 Years." *Forbes*. August 22. Accessed March 19, 2023. https://www.forbes.com/sites/bernard-marr/2022/08/22/the-top-10-most-in-demand-skills-for-the-next-10-years/?sh=5d83b02b17be.

Morgan, Jacob. 2020. ""What is leadership, and who is a leader?"." *Chief Learning Officer*. January 6. Accessed February 17, 2021. https://www.chieflearningofficer.com/2020/01/06/what-is-leadership-and-who-is-a-leader.

Mubeen, Junaid. 2017. "Mathematics must be creative, else it ain't mathematics." *A Medium Corporation*. November 19. Accessed January 4, 2019. https://medium.com/q-e-d/mathematics-must-be-creative-else-it-aint-mathematics-6c9a82e25a67.

National Endowment for the Arts. 2023. "New Data Show Economic Activity of the U.S. Arts & Cultural Sector in 2021." *National Endowment for the Arts*. March 15. Accessed March 17, 2023. https://www.arts.gov/news/press-releases/2023/new-data-show-economic-activity-us-arts-cultural-sector-2021.

Read aBannedBook, [@RetiredLibrarian]. 2023. "Spout." April 25.

Robbins Dudeck, Theresa, and Caitlin McClure, . 2018. "Applied Theatre." Methuen Drama, April 19.

Rojas, Ricardo. 2023. "A Mother's Day Greeting Card Shower for Yurok Elders." *Friends of Pine Ridge Reservation*. https://friendsofpineridgereservation.org/an-mothers-day-greeting-card-shower-for-yurok-elders/.

Taylor, Philip. 2003. *Applied Theatre: Creating Transformative Encounters in the Community.* Heinemann Drama.

Traister, Rebecca. 2018. *Good and Mad: The Revolutionar Power of Women's Anger.* New York: Simon & Schuster.

Trespicio, Terri. 2021. *Unfollow Your Passio: How to Create a Life that Matters to You.* New York: Atria.

True Sioux Hope Foundation. 2022. *Pine Ridge Statistics vs. Worldwide Statistics.* Accessed July 13, 2023. https://www.truesiouxhope.org/single-post/2015/08/21/pine-ridge-statistics-vs-worldwide-statistics.

Ulaby, Neda. 2020. "'I Am Mourning The Loss': Two-Thirds Of Artists Report They're Now Unemployed." *NPR.* April 24.

Vygotsky, Lev. 1978. "The Role of Play in Development." In *Mind in society*, by Lev Vygotsky, translated by M. Cole, 92-104. Cambridge, MA: Harvard University Press. Accessed March 16, 2023. https://www.brainyquote.com/quotes/lev_vygotsky_700802#.

Waddington-Azambuja, Alicia. 2022. "Moving from Story-telling to Story-Listening ." *Stronger Stories.* May 25. Accessed April 24, 2023. https://strongerstories.org/content-hub/moving-from-story-telling-to-story-listening/.

Wiktionary. n.d. *"Serendipty".* https://www.wordnik.com/words/serendipity.

Williamson, Rachel. 2023. "Personal Correspondance." April.

Wimalasiri, Isuri. 2017. "Serendipity: Is it mere lucky coincidence?" *Hektoen International: A Journal of Medi-*

cal Humanities. Winter. https://hekint.org/2017/01/22/serendipity-is-it-mere-lucky-coincidence/.

Wordnik. n.d. *Serendipity*. Accessed March 14, 2023. http://www.wordnik.com/words/serendipity.

www.ingramcontent.com/pod-product-compliance
Lightning Source LLC
Chambersburg PA
CBHW060252150626
46553CB00019BA/1790